BREAKING
THE
MIRACLE BARRIER

BREAKING
THE
MIRACLE BARRIER

Releasing God's Power for Breakthrough

JENNIFER LeCLAIRE

Chosen

a division of Baker Publishing Group
Minneapolis, Minnesota

Published by Chosen Books
11400 Hampshire Avenue South
Bloomington, Minnesota 55438
www.chosenbooks.com

Chosen Books is a division of
Baker Publishing Group, Grand Rapids, Michigan

Printed in the United States of America

Library of Congress Cataloging-in-Publication Data
Names: LeClaire, Jennifer (Jennifer L.), author.
Title: Breaking the miracle barrier : releasing God's power for breakthrough / Jennifer
    LeClaire.
Description: Minneapolis, Minnesota : Chosen Books, 2021.
Identifiers: LCCN 2020037990 | ISBN 9780800799366 (trade paperback) | ISBN
    9780800762162 (casebound) | ISBN 9781493430130 (ebook)
Subjects: LCSH: Miracles. | Spirituality—Christianity.
Classification: LCC BT97 .L384 2021 | DDC 234/.13—dc23
LC record available at https://lccn.loc.gov/2020037990

Some names and identifying details have been changed to protect the privacy of individuals.

21   22   23   24   25   26   27   7   6   5   4   3   2   1

I dedicate this book to Sierra Angelini, who has demonstrated what it means to stand in faith when the gates of hell are trying to prevail against her life. I am proud to call her a spiritual daughter and cannot wait to see how many captives she sets free through her ministry. Stand and keep on standing!

Contents

Contents

Acknowledgments

Thanks, as always, to the team at Chosen Books, led by Jane Campbell, that works tirelessly to ensure accuracy in the Word and Spirit. I would not have written this book without the suggestion of Jane, who heard this message and saw the potential to help the Body of Christ find new levels of breakthrough via this hidden truth throughout the pages of the Bible.

1

The Sound of Now

I needed a breakthrough. I was walking through a season of spiritual warfare, the pain of betrayal inflicted by people I would never have imagined were Judases in disguise. It was a season like nothing I had ever experienced before and hope never to experience again.

I refer to it as a "Job 1 season"—a season in which a trial comes, then another, then another, then another in rapid-fire succession. Maybe you can relate. My Job 1 season started with a freak accident that left me with a debilitating limp for months on end. I was not playing soccer or running a marathon when it happened. No, I was reading Christian books in my bright orange prayer chair just before I collapsed.

I got up to walk toward the kitchen where my brewing coffee was calling my name. I took one step, two steps. . . . On the third step, my left foot went numb, and I heard an unmistakable snap. I did not twist my ankle, nor did I turn it. I was walking on level ground, and it just snapped unexplainably. Immediately, I was in excruciating pain with a high, mid and low ankle sprain that stubbornly refused to heal. At key points in the recovery process, just as the pain started to subside, I would reinjure it and have to start all over.

Despite the torn ligaments that kept me up at night and made it difficult to walk in the day, I pressed on. Two days after the injury, I would head out to lead my first-ever intercessor's retreat in Kansas City. I refused to let those intercessors down. Rather, I would demonstrate to them the power of persevering prayer and a determined heart. Everything seemed to be moving along, until another Job-like episode occurred.

While at the retreat, I got word that the back wall of our Awakening House of Prayer (AHOP) church building in South Florida, where I pastor and lead a prayer movement in several nations, had collapsed. It was literally on the six-o'clock news on every station in our region, and later in the newspapers. I was in disbelief until I saw it online with my own two eyes. Still, I could hardly believe it.

That was when someone reminded me that Chuck Pierce, an apostle and prophet and president of Glory of Zion International Ministries in Texas, had preached at AHOP just a few months before the building collapsed and had prophesied that the walls and roof would shake and that God was going to shake us out of that place. Then he said this: "Awakening House of Prayer will be known as the house that shook." He had no idea of the extent of his words at the time. But AHOP is in fact now known around the country as the house that shook.

Our ministry was displaced for months. The enemy saw this as an opportune time to pounce and poured gas on the fiery blaze that had come to test me. People started leaving the church in droves. A hundred thousand dollars' worth of equipment that we needed to function in ministry was trapped in our church building, which the city threatened to condemn. So-called prophets sent me messages proclaiming that I was suffering the judgment of God. I started to imagine how Job felt when his friends were accusing, er, advising him during his difficulties.

As the raging trial got hotter, I chose to take a few days off and lock myself away in a hotel room to rest, pray, study and reflect. I hoped to receive some overwhelming revelation as to the root of the resistance. I wanted to understand what I was going through. I needed some aha moments that would shine a light on next steps for the ministry. I expected a prophetic dream, vision or encounter. I got none of that. God was awkwardly silent, and I grew more discouraged as the clock ticked and tocked toward Sunday morning service.

Somewhat frustrated when Sunday rolled around sooner than I had hoped, I began the drive back to Awakening House of Prayer, which was meeting at that point in a local hotel. I had a message prepared for the few people left in our congregation after the shaking. I was encouraging myself in the Lord, praying in the Spirit, and navigating interstate traffic when God finally spoke.

It was not in a still, small voice. I did not fall into a trance. A prophet did not meet me on the way. The revelation did not come through a dramatic encounter. I saw a truck with writing on the side that struck me: *The Sound of Now*. Those words were glowing with glory in the Spirit like a bright shining object I could not have ignored even if I had wanted to. I am accustomed to the Lord speaking to me through signs on billboards or bumper stickers. God can speak in many ways, and this mode of communication has been a running theme in my life. I have discovered sometimes that He speaks in unusual ways—those times when we might miss His still, small voice when vain imaginations come against our minds or incessant reasoning overwhelms our emotions.

Clearly, the Lord was sending me a message hidden in a mystery.

"What is 'the sound of now'?" I asked.

Faith is now, the Lord said.

What Is the Sound of Now?

On my way to church that morning, while praying and meditating on the Holy Spirit's "faith is now" response to my inquiry, I developed a clear message that led to massive breakthrough in my life and in the life of my church. Over the next year, as the Holy Spirit gave me more and more revelation into this mystery, I did not share it with others until I sat down to pen the pages of this book.

See, the sound of now is the sound of faith—but not just any faith. The sound of now is desperate faith that breaks the miracle barrier. The sound of now is not something you can conveniently conjure up because you need an immediate answer. The sound of now comes not from the mind. It is not an intellectual exercise or a spiritual formula you can mix on demand. The sound of now comes from the desperate heart that believes God hears and answers prayer—and you will see in the pages ahead that it manifests in many ways.

Within all the important talk among significant Bible teachers about the good fight of faith, persistent faith, enduring faith and the like, the sound of now enters as a unique expression of desperate faith. One definition of *desperate* is "having lost hope," according to Merriam-Webster,[1] and this desperation—which sits right on the edge of hopelessness—is part and parcel of the sound of now. This desperate faith—which releases the sound of now—arises only when we have lost hope in our own ability to see the prayer answer we need.

This sound manifests when we come to the end of ourselves and all our striving. It is a sound that emanates from our souls when we realize no amount of work, no amount of money—nothing but God's answer to our prayer can bring the breakthrough. It is a sound that echoes in the spirit when we finally grasp the reality that only the Breaker Himself can step into our circumstances and bend them toward His will.

Desperate faith, then, is not hopeless faith, because faith is the substance of things hoped for and the evidence of things not seen (see Hebrews 11:1). Desperate faith is faith placed in the right Person—in the Everlasting God. But desperate faith often expresses itself with desperate measures. Indeed, Merriam-Webster also defines *desperate* as "involving or employing extreme measures in an attempt to escape defeat or frustration."

What sound do you make when you are frustrated? Do you release desperate faith—the sound of now—or do you release the sound of anger at God because your hope is deferred and your heart is sick? What sound do you make when you feel defeated? Do you release desperate faith, or do you gripe about your experience? The sound of now defies our feelings as we release cries in response to what God has said instead of what the enemy is saying. This holy desperation comes from a heart that walks by faith and not by sight—and releases a sound that demands heaven's attention.

Desperate faith—the type of faith undaunted by obstacles, opposition and odds—is the very fabric of the sound of now. Desperate faith does not give up in the face of the challenge to hold on to a promise, but is supercharged with even more determination to see God's will come to pass. Desperate faith is persistent faith, then, but it does not follow that all persistent faith is desperate faith. Desperate faith has nothing left to lose except the promise—and refuses to lose at any cost.

The sound of now stems from faith that puts a demand on the Yes-and-Amen promises of God to manifest miracles. It comes from faith that understands God is not a man that He should lie, nor the son of man that He should repent (see Numbers 23:19). It comes from faith that understands God does not forsake the righteous, and He is a very present help in time of need (see Psalm 46:1). It comes from faith that knows God is no respecter of persons—what He does for one He will do for another (see Romans 2:11). As David said, "I was desperate for you to help me in my struggles, and you did!" (Psalm 120:1 TPT).

Desperate faith comes from a broken and contrite heart, and God looks upon such hearts (see Psalm 51:17). We cannot decide on a whim to release desperate faith, but we should be encouraged that when we understand how desperate we really are, we are getting close to releasing the sound of now that causes Jesus to stop dead in His tracks, look our way and ask us what we want.

The Enemy's Noise

Of the many weapons the enemy uses to diffuse the sound of now in our hearts and minds, noise in its many forms tops the list. The enemy loves to stir us to distraction with the clamoring noises around us. When we are desperately seeking instructions for breakthrough, noise steers our souls away from hearing God's voice. Technically, noise is a sound, but in the enemy's hands it is an undesired sound. It is an interfering sound. It is a disturbing sound. Noise can be a meaningless sound, but it almost always demands our attention.

The first and most obvious form is physical noise. I am easily distracted by noise. I like silence. When I write in my home office, I have to contend with any number of sounds outside my condo—from neighbors playing music too loudly to screaming sirens on the street below to hungry babies crying in the hallway.

What do I do? I fight back. I put industrial strength plugs in my ears and play rain sounds on my computer so I can drown out the background noise. When I do, I am far more focused and productive—I reach far more goals in a day—by taking measures to cut out noises that hinder my progress.

Another noise the enemy uses to distract us is the noise of the past. This is a devastating counter to desperate faith. The noise of the past is like a broken record, replaying in our minds all the times we failed, all the prayers and petitions God never seemed to answer, all the problems we have yet to overcome. The noise of the past can hinder our present and future breakthroughs.

Our heavenly Father understands how past disappointments can spark the wrong type of desperation in our hearts. This is why He tells us directly, "Do not remember the former things, nor consider the things of old. Behold, I will do a new thing, now it shall spring forth; shall you not know it? I will even make a road in the wilderness and rivers in the desert" (Isaiah 43:18–19). Like Israel, when we are in a desperate situation the enemy attacks our faith by confronting us with our past. But God wants to make a way.

Another noise, the noise of vain imaginations and its close relative, lies, can cause us to enter into the wrong kind of desperation—a hopelessness that waters down our faith. Vain imaginations and lies come from the pit of hell. They might sound like doubt, unbelief, fear, guilt, shame or condemnation. This kind of noise can convince you that God is mad at you, or that you have done something too bad to be worthy of a prayer answer. The noise of vain imaginations and lies wants to silence your faith. It is one of the enemy's chief weapons against your mind.

Thank God, He has given us instruction in His Word to combat this noise: "Casting down imaginations and every high thing that exalts itself against the knowledge of God, [bring] every thought into captivity to the obedience of Christ" (2 Corinthians 10:5 MEV).

The *Amplified Bible, Classic Edition*, of this Scripture tells us:

> [Inasmuch as we] refute arguments and theories and reasonings and every proud and lofty thing that sets itself up against the [true] knowledge of God; . . . we lead every thought and purpose away captive into the obedience of Christ (the Messiah, the Anointed One).

The Greek words here are worth in-depth study. The phrase that directs us to *cast down* the noise of lies and vain imaginations comes from the word *kathaireó*, which has a connotation of violence. Lexicons describe this action as yanking down forcefully, destroying, leaving nothing standing or in good working order.

When noisy lies and imaginations come against your mind, you must evict them with the full force of your will. You must purpose in your heart not to allow any demonic thought to stand in your mind. The Bible says to cast down *every* imagination, not some imaginations. You are not to allow any enemy-induced thought to overwhelm the sound of now.

When Not to Stay Silent

Silence is golden at times, such as when we seek relief from bothersome noise in the world around us, but silence does not produce the sound of now. Silence, by its very definition, is the absence of sound. Although there are times to "be still and know that God is God" according to Psalm 46:10, you cannot cast down imaginations in your mind and counter the other noises of the enemy without releasing a sound. The enemy would rather you stay silent than release the sound of now. He would rather you perish without the promises than get desperate, defy his noise and release your "now" faith.

Mordecai, a devout Jewish man who adopted his orphaned cousin, Hadassah, and raised her as his own daughter, understood this. When Mordecai got wind of Haman's plans to extinguish the Jewish people, "he cried out with a loud and bitter cry" (Esther 4:1). As the news spread, the Jews in the city also started releasing various sounds, including the sound of mourning, weeping and wailing (see Esther 4:3). By that time Hadassah's name had been changed to Esther, and she was the wife of King Ahasuerus. She heard about the plot and tried to ease Mordecai's fears, but he would not be comforted.

By way of messenger, Mordecai warned Esther again of the wicked plot, hoping she would approach the king even though there was a law that anyone who entered the king's inner court without an invitation could be put to death (see Esther 4:11).

Esther did not remain silent. With desperation in her heart to avoid genocide, she approached the king, found favor in his sight and released her petition. Long story short, Haman, who had orchestrated the plot against the Jews, was hanged on the gallows he had built for Mordecai. King Ahasuerus issued a decree that the Jews could defend themselves, and they destroyed their tormentors.

There are times when God will tell you to remain silent. But the sound of now demands a desperate cry and, sometimes, desperate action. Remember that faith without works is dead.

What This Sound Did in My Life

As you will recall, I was walking through a Job 1 season when the Lord revealed to me this biblical mystery that unlocks breakthrough. My ankle was severely injured; my church building had collapsed; the enemy was influencing people to "wax vicious" like Judas in my life; and more.

I did not release the sound of now when ligaments in my ankle tore; I released the sound of pain. I did not release the sound of now when my church building collapsed; I released the sound of shock. I did not release the sound of now when I was betrayed; I released the sound of anger. We release all kinds of sounds until we get desperate enough to release the sound of now.

This quote is from a sermon delivered by William Branham, the late healing evangelist from the Voice of Healing movement (renamed Christ for the Nations), and sums up the conditions that are often necessary to drive us to the kind of faith that releases the sound of now:

> Usually it takes a state of emergency to throw us into desperation. See? It's too bad it has to do that. But human beings

20

are so slothful in their mind, that it takes an emergency. Something arises, and when they do, then it—it throws them into that desperation. And really, in doing that, in desperation it brings out that real thing that you are. It shows what you're made out of in the time of desperation. It usually pulls out all the good . . . that's in you.[2]

In the throes of a Job 1 season, I grew desperate enough to release the sound of now. When I did, I saw three 24-hour breakthroughs in my life, which I will share later in this book. And I was not the only one. When I preached this impromptu Spirit-inspired message to my congregation that Sunday morning, and they understood their utter dependence on the God of hope, many of them released the sound of now and also saw "suddenlies"—those startling moments when answers to prayer finally break through—and their own 24-hour breakthroughs. Satan's noise demands your attention, but if you learn to reject that noise and release the sound of now, you will get God's attention every time, and break through the barrier to your miracle.

I am in no way saying that those who have not been healed or have not broken out of poverty or have not had a prodigal come home—or some other heart-wrenching situation—do not have the right kind of faith to see God move. I will not pretend to know why my grandmother died of cancer after my desperate intercession filled her room with such a strong presence that we were all convinced she was healed. I do not completely understand why God sometimes moves immediately and sometimes makes us walk through the fire—other than the truth that He is conforming us into the image of Christ. But I *do* know that God is God and that He is good. And I keep fighting the good fight of faith, releasing this sound of now that breaks the miracle barrier.

In the pages of this book you will come to better understand the sound of now and what it can accomplish in your life—not so you can force God's hand with feigned desperation, but so you can understand the dynamics of this precept and break the miracle barrier. The concept of the sound of now is not defined explicitly in the pages of Scripture for all to read and understand. Rather, it is veiled in the prayer lives of desperate people who are willing to release desperate cries and take desperate measures to see enemies defeated, loved ones saved, the lost delivered—to see every desire God has put on their hearts being made manifest.

2

The Art and Science of Sound

When I was a small child, old black-and-white television shows and movies were still popular as Saturday morning reruns. Along with cartoons, we watched *The Little Rascals* and Charlie Chaplain movies. Charlie Chaplain goes down in film history as one of the most important figures of the silent movie era with his screen persona of the Little Tramp.

Having no sound by definition, silent films relied on dramatic body language and facial expressions to communicate to audiences. Though they were captivating because motion pictures were altogether new, tracking with the story line of silent films demanded focus. If you got distracted for even a moment, the lack of sound could leave a major void in the motion picture experience. You might not know what was going on!

As simultaneously pioneering and entertaining as silent films were in the early 1920s, the movie industry did not take off until "talkies"—movies with sound—came on the scene. In essence, sound took over Hollywood. Adding the art and science of sound to moving pictures ultimately revolution-ized entertainment culture, creating icons like Fred Astaire, Ginger Rogers, Clint Eastwood and, in more recent years, Brad Pitt. The U.S. film industry alone is worth more than $30 billion a year, according to IBISWorld.[1] Clearly, the art and science of sound is profitable.

Can you imagine a world without sound? Maybe you have never watched a silent movie, but surely you have tried to make out what characters on a TV show are saying when the volume was too low. How about trying to glean something from a Facebook Live video when the volume on your phone is way down? It is not possible to enjoy the fullness of the visuals without the audio. While there is value in intentional silence, a world without sound—as hearing-impaired indi-viduals know—is utterly challenging.

Consider this: God did not create the world in silence. Genesis gives us a detailed record of how He created the world and everything in it. God created with the sound of His voice. Heaven is full of sounds, from angels rejoicing over lost souls coming to salvation to the four living creatures cry-ing "Holy, holy, holy," with thundering and lightning around the throne. The world is full of sounds we hear and sounds we do not hear, including ultrasonic and subsonic sound waves.

Keep this in mind: Sound never dies; it just grows fainter. The sound of Martin Luther King Jr.'s "I Have a Dream" speech is still out in the universe; the sound waves are just too indistinct for the human ear to hear. Likewise, the sound of your prayer never dies. George Washington's prayers for America are still in God's ears. Your grandmother's prayers for you are still before God's throne. God does not exist in time. Everything is present with God.

Scientists tell us there is a sound barrier—and it can be broken. That is what creates a sonic boom when objects travel through the air faster than the speed of sound. In the realm of faith, the sound of now breaks a spiritual barrier. Understanding the dynamics of sound is important to the sound-of-now revelation. If we fail to comprehend the importance of the dimensions of sound, we will not fully engage (at least not knowingly) in the benefits sound offers to those who lift up their voices and cry aloud.

Appreciating the Art of Sound

Sound art, an artistic discipline that makes sound the primary medium, is making its way into museums, including New York's Museum of Modern Art as well as galleries in London, Shanghai, Hong Kong, Paris, Stockholm, Milan, Kobe, Melbourne and Delhi.[2] While museums have traditionally been dominated by visual works, the world is demonstrating a growing appreciation for the art of sound. If you have prophetic ears, that should tell you something. God is emphasizing sound in a new way. Even the world has taken notice.

Manifesting the sound of now begins with appreciation for the art of sound. When I was a teenager, many of my friends were musicians. We listened to alternative music like the Cure and the Smiths. The Cure, in particular, created music that was complex and multilayered. My friend Jim taught me how to listen to the song while concentrating on just one instrument or just one voice at a time. As I did, I gained fuller appreciation for the dynamics and synergy of sound. If you were not intentional about discerning the sounds, you could never fully appreciate the artistry of the song.

I discovered many people did not take the time to listen—really listen—to the music they enjoyed. They appreciated the rhythm, but they never explored the depth of what the sound communicated. I discerned how the producer artfully mixed synthesizers, drums, guitars, bass, horns, violins and trumpets to create a unified sound that in turn fascinated the Cure's fans. Not everyone could articulate the artful orchestration of the sound, but the genius of the creation was mesmerizing. I gained new appreciation for the art of sound during those exercises. As a born-again believer, I have learned to place a high value on sounds in the natural and sounds in the spirit.

Clearly, God values sound—and God Himself sings (see Zephaniah 3:17). Sound existed before Adam. Angels were praising God in heaven before the earth was formed (see Nehemiah 9:6). Lucifer was making music before the fall of the angels (see Ezekiel 28:13). The sons of God shouted for joy after God laid the foundations of the earth (see Job 38:7). Sound is so important to creation that God created sound before He created man, the seas, the plants and the animals.

God created everything with the sound of His words. He uses sound to communicate to humankind and to enable humankind—and animals—to communicate with each other. We should appreciate sound because God created it. When we appreciate something, we recognize its value. When we recognize the value of something, we pay attention to it. When we pay attention to something, we can reap greater rewards from it.

Searching Out the Science of Sound

The art and power of sound is based on the science of sound, which is also fascinating. Simply stated, sound is created when energy is released in vibration form. Sound travels in waves that essentially move air and vibrate parts of your ear. Scientists have proved that sound also moves matter.

A Royal Horticultural Society study concluded that talking to your plants can help them grow faster. And what is said to the plants matters. Swedish-based furniture company IKEA conducted a study in which children were instructed to bully two identical plants with (with identical light and water conditions) and praise another every day for thirty days. At the end of the experiment, the bullied plant had a starkly different appearance. Its leaves were droopy and dying. Many similar studies support these results.[3]

Like humans, plants are living organisms that God created. Like plants, humans are made up mostly of water. Scientists tell us that sound not only moves through water but actually changes its structure. I was traveling in Taiwan and walking on that badly injured ankle I told you about. I was in so much pain my hosts took me to the doctor. While I was waiting for my X rays, the doctor showed me an album of photos of water compiled by Japanese scientist Masaru Emoto.

Emoto's studies show that our words have dramatic effects on water. After reading the Bible and praying out loud—or speaking positive words—to water and freezing it, the water formed beautiful crystal shapes. Speaking negative words to the water formed small, ugly crystalized shapes when the water was frozen.[4] And that is not the only science we have to lean on that proves the power of sound.

In December 2019 I read a story about surgeons who performed a cardiac catheterization using sound waves. That's right, sound waves. A company called Shockwave Medical developed the equipment. According to an article in United With Israel,

> The treatment entails the deployment of a tiny balloon filled with fluid and tiny balls at the point where there is a build-up of calcium within the artery. After the balloon is in place, sound waves are triggered to create a rapid movement of the balls which create cracks in the calcium inside the artery. . . .
>
> Catheterization has previously not been possible in complex cases of calcium accumulation in the arteries since any intervention would have caused damage or rupture of the artery. As a result, patients suffering from congestive arterial congestion had to undergo complex bypass surgery to overcome the problem.
>
> Dr. Yaron Almagor, Director of the Catheterization Unit at Sha'are Zedek, stated that the new method is "significant news for many patients who have up until now had to undergo complex treatments and surgeries."[5]

That is how powerful sound is. Sound is saving lives in more ways than one.

We also know sound can move matter. In the summer of 2018, after our ministry building collapsed, one of our pastors told me that a vibrating sound had been shaking the walls. For some weeks prior, he had dealt with a buzzing noise that was distracting him from a filming project. He could never figure out what it was. Then one day the building suddenly collapsed.

Insurance investigators finally determined that the heavy equipment operation, blasting and drilling on the condo development next to us had actually caused waves of vibration in the ground that shook our foundation. It reminds me of how the shout of the Israelites shook the walls of Jericho down, which we will talk about in a later chapter.

Sound is a vital part of survival on many levels. Think of fire alarms or approaching sirens. What if no one could hear you scream if you were in danger? Without sound, a crying baby could not communicate her needs with her parents. While scientists say we need silence to survive, we also need sound. When we are desperate to break through the miracle barrier, silence does not communicate that desperation—sound does.

The Power of Sound

Sounds carry power—either creative or destructive.

Our sounds can produce death or life (see Proverbs 18:21). God created the universe with words—with sounds. We create our worlds with words—with sounds. Put another way, while our thoughts fuel our inner lives, our words shape our outer lives.

Our words can agree with God or with the enemy. When we make "God sounds"—when we speak His words—we are creating (or recreating) our realities. We are setting the stage for breakthrough. God's Word does not return to Him void but accomplishes what He sent it to do (see Isaiah 55:11). We can send God's Word to accomplish His will through the sounds from our holy mouths.

Jesus is the High Priest of our profession (see Hebrews 3:1). Keep in mind the Greek word for *profession* in this verse is *homologia*, which means "what one professes [confesses]," according to *The KJV New Testament Greek Lexicon*.[6] *Strong's Exhaustive Concordance* defines *profession* as "to say the same thing about."[7] God wants us to say the same thing about our lives that He is saying—even if our lives do not currently match the promises.

If we want to tap into the sound of now, we have to say the same things that God is saying about our lives now. God's perspective is different from ours. He sees us through the saving blood of Jesus Christ. He sees our ending from our beginning. God can "call into being things that don't even exist yet" (Romans 4:17 TPT). The *Amplified Bible, Classic Edition*, expounds on this concept, explaining how God "speaks of the nonexistent things that [He has foretold and promised] as if they [already] existed."

Kenneth Hagin recounts a revelation he received regarding John 14:13, which reads, "And whatever you ask in My name, that I will do, that the Father may be glorified in the Son."

Hagin explains that he was once part of a group of young ministers whom a Hebrew and Greek scholar was addressing. The scholar explained that there are Greek and Hebrew words for which we have no idiom in the English language. He addressed John 14:13 as an example.

"Now, the translators felt they ought to use either 'I will' or 'I shall,'" [said the scholar], "because that is the strongest assertion you can make in the English language. You can't say anything stronger than 'I will do it,' or 'I shall do it.'"

The scholar then read the verse in Greek and said: "This is what that verse literally says: 'If you will ask anything in My Name, if I don't have it, I'll make it for you!'"

Hagin exclaimed, "'I'll make it for you!' Thank God, He can, because He is El Shaddai—the God who is more than enough!"[8]

The power of life in our words can move God to create whatever it is we need to fulfill His promises in our lives and bring us into breakthrough. The sound of now—seen in art, proven in science—shifts realities.

3

Discovering the Sound of God

Elijah knew the sound of God's voice. Jehovah gave the prophet instructions time and time again—and he obeyed with success. But in times of distress, it often seems more difficult to hear the sound of God, does it not?

You remember the story. Elijah called for a showdown at Mount Carmel with the false prophets of Baal. Elijah put them to open shame and the Israelites who witnessed God's power-and-fire display turned their hearts back to the Lord as King Ahab watched from a distance, surely awestruck. When Ahab told Jezebel what had happened at Mount Carmel, the wicked queen sent a messenger with a death threat to Elijah. The powerful prophet feared for his life and ran to hide in a cave.

I believe the Lord spoke to Elijah in the midst of his desperate running, but Elijah was so fearful of Jezebel's witchcraft that he could not think straight, see straight or hear straight (see 2 Kings 9:22). It was not God's will for Elijah to run from Jezebel but rather to overthrow her. We find

Elijah isolated in his cave when God met him there. Read the account in 1 Kings 19:9–13 (NIV):

> The word of the LORD came to him: "What are you doing here, Elijah?"
>
> He replied, "I have been very zealous for the LORD God Almighty. The Israelites have rejected your covenant, torn down your altars, and put your prophets to death with the sword. I am the only one left, and now they are trying to kill me too."
>
> The LORD said, "Go out and stand on the mountain in the presence of the LORD, for the LORD is about to pass by."
>
> Then a great and powerful wind tore the mountains apart and shattered the rocks before the LORD, but the LORD was not in the wind. After the wind there was an earthquake, but the LORD was not in the earthquake. After the earthquake came a fire, but the LORD was not in the fire. And after the fire came a gentle whisper. When Elijah heard it, he pulled his cloak over his face and went out and stood at the mouth of the cave.

Although Elijah did not hear God's voice while running from Jezebel, when the battle ceased the prophet was able to discern God's sound. He knew the Lord was not in the wind, earthquake or fire. He waited for the gentle whisper, the still, small voice, and then he heard the quiet instruction to anoint Jehu, who would take Jezebel down, and Elisha, whom he could raise up to succeed him.

Desperation is one ingredient in the sound of now; hearing the sound of God's voice and discerning the sound of His movements are also keys to releasing the right sound at the right time. When we pray what God tells us to pray when He tells us to pray it, we are setting ourselves up for miracle breakthrough results.

Hearing the Sound of God's Voice

Jesus said, "My sheep hear My voice" (John 10:27). But what does God's voice sound like? When you watch Christian films or listen to audio versions of the Bible, you hear many renditions of God's voice. For Cecil B. DeMille's epic *The Ten Commandments*, Charlton Heston, who played Moses, later revealed that he had also supplied God's deep voice. The movie *Exodus: Gods and Kings* cast an eleven-year-old British schoolboy as the voice of God. In the animated *The Prince of Egypt*, Val Kilmer also played the double role of Moses and God.

The sound of God's voice might come in that still, small speech Elijah heard, or it might come in a more dramatic form as it did when John baptized Jesus in the Jordan River, and a voice from heaven said, "This is My beloved Son, in whom I am well pleased" (Matthew 3:17).

The Bible often describes God's voice as mighty. Ezekiel heard God's voice as the sound of many waters (see Ezekiel 43:2). John the Beloved echoed Ezekiel's experience in Revelation 1:15. Daniel described the sound of God's words as "the voice of a multitude" (Daniel 10:6). Psalm 29:3–4 gives us a dramatic description of God's voice: "The voice of the LORD is over the waters; the God of glory thunders; the LORD is over many waters. The voice of the LORD is powerful; the voice of the LORD is full of majesty."

God's voice sometimes does not make a sound that we hear with our ears. Sometimes we perceive a flash of understanding without words. You just know that you know that you know that God is speaking to you even though you cannot hear His voice. This inspiration surpasses your natural reasoning. It is a knowing in your inner person—in your spirit. In the same way, God speaks through faint impressions

33

telling you to do or say something. An urging or prompting in your spirit leads you. This is the Holy Spirit's work in you.

Likewise, the sound of God's voice manifests through wisdom and common sense. James 1:5 promises this: "If any of you lacks wisdom, let him ask of God, who gives to all liberally and without reproach, and it will be given to him." In these instances God's voice resonates as wisdom in your soul or wise counsel through other people who have the mind of God.

God's voice sometimes sounds like the peace in your heart that passes all understanding. Consider Paul's Spirit-inspired words in Colossians 3:15 (AMPC):

Let the peace (soul harmony which comes) from Christ rule (act as umpire continually) in your hearts [deciding and settling with finality all questions that arise in your minds, in that peaceful state] to which as [members of Christ's] one body you were also called [to live]. And be thankful (appreciative), [giving praise to God always].

Peace should always rule your decision-making—just as an umpire rules whether or not a pitched ball is in or out of the strike zone.

God's voice often manifests through dreams and visions. God has been using dreams and visions to speak to His people since the Book of Beginnings—that is, the book of Genesis. From Genesis to Revelation, God speaks through dreams and visions. As Acts 2:17 reveals, "It shall come to pass in the last days, says God, that I will pour out of My Spirit on all flesh; your sons and your daughters shall prophesy, your young men shall see visions, your old men shall dream dreams." Dreams and visions are increasing these days, but many times we do not know what God is saying through them. We have to press into these revelations for, as Proverbs 25:2 explains, "It is the glory of God to conceal a matter, but the glory of kings is to search out a matter."

He can speak through your circumstances. At times, relationships fizzle, doors close, opportunities dry up. That could be God's way of showing you that transition is here, and it is time to move on. God told the prophet Elijah, for example, to go down to the Brook Cherith to find provision before the famine came (see 1 Kings 17). Eventually, the brook dried up. But notice that the brook dried up before God spoke to him to move on to Zarephath (see verses 7–9). When things are drying up, God could be speaking that it is time to move.

When people reject our business proposals, reject our marriage proposals or otherwise say no, we can feel disappointed, discouraged or dejected. We later realize that God was speaking to us not to connect with that business partner, that would-be spouse or the one who said no. We felt dejected at the time, but later we see that we were protected by the hand of God. This is circumstantial speaking.

And God speaks, of course, through Scripture. When you cannot hear God speaking any other way, pick up your Bible and keep reading it until you have the revelation you need. Often when you read God's Word and talk to Him about what it says, He will speak to you about your circumstances either directly or through the Scriptures.

Discerning the Sound of God's Movements

The first mention of sound in the Bible refers to God's movement in the Garden of Eden: "They heard the sound of the LORD God walking in the garden in the cool of the day, and the man and his wife hid themselves from the presence of the LORD God among the trees of the garden" (Genesis 3:8 ESV).

God makes a sound when He moves, which might be heard in either the physical realm or the spiritual realm. We need to cultivate sensitivity to His heart to discern His movement and move with Him. Although the sound of now can release instant breakthrough, sometimes we must wait for just the right moment to release the sound. "Just the right moment" is when God moves in our midst or tells us "now." This is illustrated in 1 Chronicles 14:15 when God told David not to enter into battle until he heard the sound of marching in the tops of the mulberry trees.

Jesus compared the movement of the Holy Spirit to wind and said, "You hear the sound of it" (John 3:8). When God the Holy Spirit came at Pentecost, there was the sound of a mighty rushing wind. Just as you can see the effect of blowing wind, you can see (or hear) the evidence of a moving God.

Psalm 29:5–9 gives us a dramatic description of the visual effects of God's movement:

> The voice of the LORD breaks the cedars, yes, the LORD splinters the cedars of Lebanon. He makes them also skip like a calf, Lebanon and Sirion like a young wild ox. The voice of the LORD divides the flames of fire.
>
> The voice of the LORD shakes the wilderness; the LORD shakes the Wilderness of Kadesh. The voice of the LORD makes the deer give birth, and strips the forests bare; and in His temple everyone says, "Glory!"

Psalm 46:6 tells us that when God raises His voice, the earth melts.

You have probably heard it said, "God moves in mysterious ways." God never intended for His ways to be altogether mysterious to His children. We can study the ways of God and learn them from practical experience. In fact, the ability to discern the sound of God's movements is often rooted in understanding how He moves—His ways. This can take diligent study because God's ways are not our ways (see Isaiah 55:8). David cried, "Teach me Your way, O Lord, and lead me in a smooth path, because of my enemies" (Psalm 27:11).

The Sound of Silence

Beyond appreciating the art and science of sound, and understanding the potential detrimental effects of noise, we need to appreciate the sound of silence—not God's silence but our own. My journey in understanding the value of a still soul—of being still and knowing He is God (see Psalm 46:10)—has positioned me to release the sound of now with precise timing. Desperation mixed with confidence in a good God inspires us to release sound that reaches the throne even when bronze heavens make us feel as if our prayers are not ascending beyond the ceiling.

Sometimes discerning the sound of God (or the sound of God's movement or voice) requires waiting—sometimes even waiting in silence until we discern His presence and hear Him speak above our noisy thoughts and the enemy's vain imaginations. There are times when God seems silent—and sometimes He is—but I have learned this: If I get silent, I will often hear Him talking. Sometimes the issue is not that He is silent but that our souls are too noisy for our spiritual ears to hear Him.

Maybe you feel like Job when he lamented in the midst of his fiery trial, "I cry out to You, but You do not answer me" (Job 30:20). Maybe you can relate to David's frustration when he wrote, "This You have seen, O LORD; do not keep silence" (Psalm 35:22). Sometimes God's silence feels painful, but it does not have to be.

When we make Psalm 62:5 our reality—"My soul, wait silently for God alone, for my expectation is from Him"—we will not grow frustrated and our faith will not waiver. When we choose to walk in Psalm 37:7 (NIV)—"Be still before the LORD and wait patiently for Him"—we will not be disappointed in the results. Stand on Psalm 50:3: "Our God shall come, and shall not keep silent."

Yes, at times God is silent. God may be silent because we are. The Holy Spirit sometimes waits for us to initiate the conversation. God may be silent because we did not obey His last instruction, and He is waiting for us to be willing and obedient so we can eat the good of the land. God may be silent because we are practicing sin, and He is waiting for us to repent. God may be silent because He has given us the answer in His Word, and He wants us to study to show ourselves approved (see 2 Timothy 2:15).

God may be silent because we ask for the wrong things in prayer or pray with the wrong motives. God may be silent because He has already answered, and there is a war in the heavens over the delivery of our answers. God may be silent because He has already answered, and we failed to recognize the sound of His voice. God may be silent because He is stretching our faith. God may be silent because we are not ready to hear the answer.

What to Do When God Is Silent

When God is silent, the first thing I do is read His Word. Bill Johnson taught me to "read until He speaks." Paul shared a similar secret with Timothy: "All Scripture is given by inspiration of God, and is profitable for doctrine, for reproof, for correction, for instruction in righteousness, that the man of God may be complete, thoroughly equipped for every good work" (2 Timothy 3:16–17). Even if you still cannot hear God speaking, when you read the Word, you are renewing your mind and strengthening your spirit.

I never like when God is silent; I never pray expecting not to get a response. Once I was trying to make a decision about a project that I no longer enjoyed. I felt no grace in it. I was almost at the point of resentment. I felt trapped. I knew I could not shut it down, but I did not want to continue the exercise of beating my head against a wall.

Finally, after a season of silence and after pledging to the Lord that I would do His will if I just knew what it was, He said one thing, *Stop kicking against the pricks*. This is what He told Paul when Paul thought he was doing the will of God but was actually resisting God's will unknowingly (see Acts 26:14). In my case, God had been silent waiting for me to see what should have been obvious, and finally spoke as I studied the Word. See, I saw the project as a thorn in my side. I was focusing on pricks, but I did not know I was kicking against them. I had to repent.

When God is silent, repent of any known wrongdoing or disobedience. When God is silent, go back and look at any prophetic words spoken over your life or any promises God has given you—then meditate on them, confess them and war with them according to 1 Timothy 1:18. When God is silent, ask Him for wisdom, because He has promised in His Word to pour it out liberally (see James 1:5). You might not hear His voice, but you can receive wisdom in other ways. When God is silent, continue to acknowledge Him in all your ways with trust that He will direct your paths (see Proverbs 3:6). When God is silent, ask for counsel from those who have a different perspective.

The next time God seems silent, do not be afraid to ask Him why. He might not tell you, but then again He might. Remember, His ways are not our ways. He is a good God, and His intentions toward you are kind. Keep talking to Him, even if He is not talking to you. Trust in Him, even in the silence, and you will hear the sound of His voice showing you the path to breakthrough at the perfect time.

Keep in mind these profound words of Oswald Chambers:

Are you mourning before God because you have not had an audible response? When you cannot hear God, you will find that He has trusted you in the most intimate way possible— with absolute silence, not a silence of despair, but one of pleasure, because He saw that you could withstand an even bigger revelation. If God has given you a silence, then praise Him—He is bringing you into the mainstream of His purposes. The actual evidence of the answer in time is simply a matter of God's sovereignty. Time is nothing to God.[1]

4

Engaging a Sound-Activated Kingdom

Apple's Siri, Google's Assistant and Amazon's Alexa are all part of my everyday life. I live in a sound-activated house, a sound-activated car—a sound-activated world—and so do you. You can turn on your lights with a clap, turn on your thermostat with your voice, turn on your TV or play music without pressing a button. And the list goes on.

It is convenient, even if it is not perfect. We can be thankful that God and His angels hear us perfectly! Unfortunately, so does the enemy of our souls when we speak out loud.

The Kingdom of God is a sound-activated kingdom. God's sound activated the creation of the earth, and your sound activates creations in your life. Put another way, the power of death and life are in the tongue (see Proverbs 18:21). God knows it, the devil knows it, and we need to know it—really know it.

The New Living Translation puts it this way: "The tongue can bring death or life." The Contemporary English Version says: "Words can bring death or life!" The Good News

Translation tells us: "What you say can preserve life or destroy it." *The Message* asserts: "Words kill, words give life." And the Passion Translation states plainly: "Your words are so powerful that they will kill or give life, and the talkative person will reap the consequences." No matter how you translate it, you can see that sound activates your harvest.

I have read every known translation of this verse and have noticed something to which we need to pay close attention: Death is almost always listed before life. I believe that is because God is warning us how the enemy will use our words against us—and I have witnessed how many Christians activate death in their lives through the power of their words. Every day we are engaging in a sound-activated Kingdom whether or not we are aware of the consequences.

Before we correlate the sound-activated Kingdom to sound-of-now miracle breakthroughs, it is literally life-and-death critical that we understand the power of the sounds we create. Remember, God created the entire world and everything in it—including humankind—with His sounds. Think about it this way: You are creating your future now with your sound. Your sound cannot change your past, but your sound can create your now and your future now.

What Sound Are You Creating?

Will you accept the challenge to listen to the sound you are creating and consider the consequences? Will you examine the fruit of your sounds? Will you change the way you think about the sounds you make so you can see different outcomes?

Jesus made it plain: "I say to you that for every idle word men may speak, they will give account of it in the day of judgment. For by your words you will be justified, and by your words you will be condemned" (Matthew 12:36–37).

You might wonder what Jesus qualifies as an idle word. *Idle* means "inactive, not turned to normal or appropriate use, lacking worth or basis, vain," according to the dictionary. And according to *Strong's*, *idle* speaks of words that are "thoughtless, unprofitable and injurious." With this in mind, take a moment to think about the sound that your words create. Are your words making inappropriate worthless, thoughtless, unprofitable and injurious sounds? Or are they making valuable, thoughtful, profitable and healing sounds?

Do you need to repent? Do you need to change the way you think about how you speak? Jesus said, "Out of the fullness (the overflow, the superabundance) of the heart the mouth speaks" (Matthew 12:34 AMPC). The Passion Translation puts it this way: "What has been stored up in your hearts will be heard in the overflow of your words!" If you have a mouth issue, you have a heart issue. If you have a heart issue, you are probably releasing a sound of now that will open the door for the enemy to bring death and destruction into your life.

Jesus also said that our words can justify or condemn us. This is in line with the power of life and death coming out of our mouths. The *KJV New Testament Greek Lexicon* tells us that *justify* in this verse means "to render righteous." *Condemn* means "to declare to be reprehensible, wrong or evil usually after weighing evidence and without reservation."

You might be saying, "But there is 'no condemnation to those who are in Christ.'" That is absolutely what Romans 8:1 says, *in part*. The full verse says this: "There is therefore now no condemnation to those who are in Christ Jesus, who do not walk according to the flesh, but according to the Spirit." When you are speaking idle words, you are not walking in the Spirit. You are walking in the flesh. God is not condemning you, but the enemy will.

It is still true that Jesus did not come into the world to condemn people. He is not doing the condemning here. This is purely self-condemnation. Nothing can separate us from God's love, but we will nevertheless have to stand before God one day and give an account for the idle words. Better to repent now so we do not have to repent later. Better to get to the heart issues now that are causing us to release sounds that are opening the door to the enemy in our lives.

Jesus said, "Those things which proceed out of the mouth come from the heart, and they defile a man" (Matthew 15:18). Again, He said, "A good man out of the good treasure of his heart brings forth good; and an evil man out of the evil treasure of his heart brings forth evil. For out of the abundance of the heart his mouth speaks" (Luke 6:45).

Solomon, inspired by the Holy Spirit, once said, "Whoever guards his mouth and tongue keeps his soul from troubles" (Proverbs 21:23). In the context of Matthew 12, can you see how the sound you make with your anointed mouth can bring your soul troubles? Solomon also said, "He who guards his mouth preserves his life, but he who opens wide his lips shall have destruction" (Proverbs 13:3).

David understood this. Meditate on these verses to help you remember to watch your sounds. Psalm 141:3 says, "Set a guard, O LORD, over my mouth; keep watch over the door of my lips." And Psalm 19:14 says, "Let the words of my mouth and the meditation of my heart be acceptable in Your sight, O LORD, my strength and my Redeemer." Amen.

Releasing Profitable Words

Of course, not all idle words are purely evil; some are just unproductive. God wants us to release the sound of now. He wants us to release words that are productive in the spiritual realm so that we can shift circumstances in the natural realm. Releasing the Word of God, for example, is a productive way to use your mouth. Hebrews 4:12 assures us that "the word of God is living and powerful, and sharper than any two-edged sword, piercing even to the division of soul and spirit, and of joints and marrow, and is a discerner of the thoughts and intents of the heart."

When we release God's words out of our mouths, we are establishing God's will in the earth because His word is His will. God Himself said this in Isaiah 55:11: "So shall My word be that goes forth from My mouth; It shall not return to Me void, but it shall accomplish what I please, and it shall prosper in the thing for which I sent it." When we send God's word, our words are profitable and creative and setting the stage for the sound of now to bring breakthrough.

We find in Job 22:28 the power of a decree to bring breakthrough: "Thou shalt also decree a thing, and it shall be established unto thee: and the light shall shine upon thy ways."

Let me show you the power of profitable words by returning to the story of our building collapsing.

It was early August 2018, and I was hosting an intercessory prayer retreat in Kansas City when I got word of the destruction. In the midst of the Job 1 trials, I was at least able to find a little levity. When one of our members told us that we were all over the news, I joked with my staff: "Awesome! It's about time the community recognizes our good works!"

But there was actually precious little to laugh about. We were displaced; we could not access our media, worship and office equipment; faithful members were leaving; we had no clue where to go or what to do.

Later, on August 16, I was sitting in my prayer chair asking the Lord what was going on and also seeking further revelation about "the sound of now," the words that had been emblazoned for me on the side of that truck I saw going down the highway as I was driving to church—right before I released the pivotal message on which this book is based.

The Lord reminded me of the prophetic word Chuck Pierce had spoken at our church. As you will recall, Chuck prophesied that the walls and roof would shake and that God was going to shake us out of that place. We all agreed it meant a spiritual shaking. But it was, first, a natural shaking.

Then finally God spoke to me: *It's good you have so many intercessors praying over this issue. But you need to get up and take charge.*

See, there are times when kings send soldiers into battle, and there are times when kings lead them into battle. The Lord was charging me with leading this battle.

I got up and began to speak decrees for two hours. (I have written extensively about the power of decrees in the believer's life.)[1] Suddenly, something came out of my mouth that shocked me: "I decree that on or before August 18, 2018, we will have papers for our new building, in the name of Jesus."

I was stunned. Our staff and equipment had been cramped in a two-thousand-square-foot building for six and a half years. We had searched high and low for an affordable, suitable facility but always came up empty. Our searching left us feeling as though we were wandering around in the wilderness. We could not find anything anywhere, largely due to zoning. It seems that in south Florida zoning officials would rather approve condos and retail facilities than churches.

I was glad nobody had heard my decree because it was unbelievable. How would we have papers on a new building in two days? I determined not to tell anyone, but the Lord told me to keep decreeing it.

I asked the Lord, "How am I supposed to find this building, Lord?"

He said, *Go look on Craigslist*.

"Craigslist?"

There was silence. I obeyed. I found a listing within fifteen minutes that was perfect for our church.

It was not available.

The broker said that it was already secured for a charter school, but he added they were having trouble getting the permit. Do you know why? Because that was my building.

On August 18, 2018, we signed a letter of intent for the new building, and the landlord approved it. Our old building had one six-by-six-foot office we all shared, no children's facility and two bathrooms. Our new facility is ten thousand square feet with rooms for the infants, children and youth, a TV studio, classrooms, a security room, several offices, bathrooms, as well as a green room and storage areas. The decree shifted an impossible circumstance and brought AHOP out of the wilderness and into its promised land.

The Sound of Your Prayer

Now let's bring this closer to the sound of now revelation. What is the big deal about sound? Why not just release your faith with internal prayers between you and God? Of course, God hears all our prayers, and there is value in praying to God silently from your heart. But words are containers of power, and sound shifts atmospheres. Jesus connected mountain-moving, miracle-working breakthrough faith to voice-activated prayers.

> Jesus answered them, "Have faith in God. For truly I say to you, whoever says to this mountain, 'Be removed and be thrown into the sea,' and does not doubt in his heart, but believes that what he says will come to pass, he will have whatever he says. Therefore I say to you, whatever things you ask when you pray, believe that you will receive them, and you will have them. And when you stand praying, forgive if you have anything against anyone, so that your Father who is in heaven may also forgive you your sins."
>
> Mark 11:22–25 MEV

Abraham called those things that were not as though they were, and they became. He did not only think about things as though they were—he called them into existence in the same way God created the world: with words. In a sound-activated Kingdom, doesn't it make sense that we would pray out loud? Sound creates, so while it is not wrong to pray in your head to God, if you need to create new realities, you should release the sound of your voice until you hear the sound of now.

Jesus prayed aloud (see John 17; Matthew 26:39). In Acts 4:24 the young Church prayed aloud. David often prayed the prayers in his psalms out loud, according to Bible historians. I like to pray the Word out loud because it builds my faith. Romans 10:17 assures us that "faith comes by hearing, and hearing by the word of God." My faith activates the promises of God through my voice.

Since praying is talking to God, praying out loud makes sense from a relational perspective. Although God can hear our internal prayers, talking to Him out loud makes it more real to me. (I never talk to my friends in my head; I speak the words out loud.) And with regard to spiritual warfare prayer, praying out loud is a must. You cannot bind the devil in your head. You have to speak out the prayer, decree or declaration into the atmosphere. In the wilderness, Jesus did not have an internal conversation with the devil. Three times He spoke aloud, "It is written" (see Matthew 4:1–11).

Romans 8:26 tells us this: "Likewise the Spirit also helps in our weaknesses. For we do not know what we should pray for as we ought, but the Spirit Himself makes intercession for us with groanings which cannot be uttered." This is not saying that groaning is expressed without making a noise: You cannot groan silently. The word *uttered* in this verse just means that it is not expressed in words—at least not natural words. Evidence of the baptism with the Holy Spirit is a heavenly prayer language that is spoken forth.

When you prayed the prayer of salvation, you did not do it in your head. The Bible required that you activate your salvation with a sound from your mouth: "If you confess with your mouth the Lord Jesus and believe in your heart that God has raised Him from the dead, you will be saved" (Romans 10:9). Confessing and believing is how we receive many things from God, even after salvation.

Praying out loud is part of activating God's purposes and will in your life. So stop and think about it: What is your sound activating? Is it activating the enemy's plan, or is it activating breakthrough?

5

The Sound of Now Captures God's Attention

When my daughter was a little girl, she got my attention simply because of who she was. I loved her unconditionally whether she was making a mess, getting good grades, having a bad attitude or doing her chores. In other words, my love for her caused me to pay attention to everything she did—good or bad.

When she fell down and skinned her knees and cried out, I was the first one there to pick her up. When she was shut away in her bedroom with a broken heart, I was the first one to comfort her. When she cried out in fear, I was the first one there to defend her.

God always sees us. He is a very present help in time of need (see Psalm 46:1). He watches over us carefully. But there is a sound that captures His attention—crying aloud. Cries carry a sense of urgency that other forms of communication do not voice.

Yes, my daughter had my attention no matter what she did, but when she cried aloud, I came running. She cried out to me because she knew I could help her. She knew Mommy could make it all better—or at least ease the pain. She knew Mom could rescue her from dangerous or distressing situations she found herself in—and she knew that I not only could but actually would.

In the same way, we always have God's attention, but when we cry aloud He hears our cries and comes to our aid speedily. But let me be clear—it is not just any crying aloud that He responds to. Although He collects our tears in a bottle, He reaches down to deliver when we cry aloud in faith. That desperation releases the sound of now and breaks the miracle barrier.

Because David walked with this heart posture, he understood that the Lord hears when the righteous cry out, and that He delivers them out of all their troubles (see Psalm 34:17). And again: "When I cry out to You, then my enemies will turn back; this I know, because God is for me" (Psalm 56:9). And again: "I will cry out to God Most High, to God who performs all things for me" (Psalm 57:2). And again: "They cry out to the LORD in their trouble, and He brings them out of their distresses" (Psalm 107:28).

Understand that the Hebrew word for *cry out* in these verses is not a self-pity-fueled weeping. *Strong's* reveals the power in this cry. It means "to utter a loud sound, to call (with the name of God) and to summon." This is not a quiet cry or even sobbing. This is a desperate loud sound that summons God to the scene to deliver the one He loves from distress. Throughout Scripture, we find people "crying out" and "crying aloud" to get God's attention—and they experience sudden breakthrough.

Blind but Noisy

Jesus does not move because we beg—no matter how much we beg. Jesus stops and listens when we release the sound of now. Indeed, Scripture gives an account of how the sound of now caused Jesus to stop dead in His tracks and take notice—then take action. We read the dramatic account in Mark 10:46–52:

> Now they came to Jericho. As He went out of Jericho with His disciples and a great multitude, blind Bartimaeus, the son of Timaeus, sat by the road begging. And when he heard that it was Jesus of Nazareth, he began to cry out and say, "Jesus, Son of David, have mercy on me!"
>
> Then many warned him to be quiet; but he cried out all the more, "Son of David, have mercy on me!" So Jesus stood still and commanded him to be called. Then they called the blind man, saying to him, "Be of good cheer. Rise, He is calling you."
>
> And throwing aside his garment, he rose and came to Jesus. So Jesus answered and said to him, "What do you want Me to do for you?" The blind man said to Him, "Rabboni, that I may receive my sight." Then Jesus said to him, "Go your way; your faith has made you well." And immediately he received his sight and followed Jesus on the road.

Let's explore the dynamics of what really happened in the spiritual realm in this scene. Jesus went out with His disciples and a large crowd. Surely, it was noisy. Where there is a great multitude, there are many sounds that accompany it. If you have ever been in a full restaurant, for example, it can be hard to hear your dinner companions over the clamor.

Before Jesus entered the city, Bartimaeus was begging. Again, we can beg God all day long, but begging does not necessarily spur God to action. Bartimaeus was likely barely getting by with his begging—and he certainly was not finding any healing power in it. Begging shows desperation, but it does not necessarily demonstrate faith that produces the sound of now. There was something, though, about the sound of the blind man's cry that stopped Jesus in His tracks. Before we explore that, notice something else.

When Bartimaeus cried out to Jesus, his buddies tried to shut him up. You can expect this reaction from some of your friends and family when you get desperate enough to release the sound of now. Some translations of the Bible reveal that people scolded him, addressed him angrily and even rebuked him for crying out to Jesus. You may get rebuked for your fervent faith on your way to breaking the miracle barrier, but take a page from the story of Bartimaeus and keep crying aloud anyway.

I know Bartimaeus was glad he did. What happens next is astounding. Jesus heard Bartimaeus's cry above all the other noise on the path. Jesus heard the sound of now—and He stopped, commanded and healed. Jesus asked the blind man what he wanted, which seems like an obvious question. God does not ask what we want or what we need because He does not *know* what we want or what we need. God knows everything. God wants us to verbalize it because with the sound of our petition we release our "now faith" in the only One who can deliver the breakthrough.

Earlier, I explained what *cry out* means in Hebrew. You might wonder what *cry out* means in Greek. Again, this is not weeping, which is another element of the sound of now that we will discuss in a later chapter. This cry means "to call aloud (shriek, exclaim, entreat), to speak with a loud voice, to cry or pray for vengeance," according to *Strong's*. This is a passionate, loud cry that entreats the Lord of breakthrough to break in now.

Bartimaeus's cry is the same intensity of the cry of the blind men following Jesus that we read about in Matthew 9:27. Both of those men were also healed. This is the same cry the father with the demonized boy issued when he cried out, with tears, "I believe; help my unbelief!" (Mark 9:24). His son was delivered immediately from a demon that had plagued him since he was a small child. *Crying out* in Scripture speaks of a strong, loud emotion. It is like putting an exclamation mark at the beginning and end of your prayer.

God Hears Our Cries

When my daughter was a baby, I could hear her cry even if I was in the deepest of sleeps. Her cries woke me up. I could discern her cry from any other baby's cry—and I always dropped everything I was doing and ran to her immediately to ease her distress. God, of course, never sleeps or slumbers (see Psalm 121:4). Though it may feel at times as if God does not hear your desperate cries for breakthrough, He does. Let me build your faith by showing you this in the Word.

Psalm 34:17 assures us of this: "The righteous cry out, and the LORD hears, and delivers them out of all their troubles." Even if you caused the trouble, you can cry out in repentance and cry out for help, and the Lord will deliver you. No matter what you have done to get yourself into a mess, God will not turn His back on you. You can approach His throne of grace boldly to find help and obtain mercy in a time of need (see Hebrews 4:16). He is that good.

You can see His goodness in Exodus 2:23–25:

> Now it happened in the process of time that the king of Egypt died. Then the children of Israel groaned because of the bondage, and they cried out; and their cry came up to God because of the bondage. So God heard their groaning, and God remembered His covenant with Abraham, with Isaac, and with Jacob. And God looked upon the children of Israel, and God acknowledged them.

The Lord raised up a deliverer because of the Israelites' cries. In the book of Judges, we see Israel commit spiritual adultery and follow after other gods over and over until they were conquered and put into bondage by their enemies. But when the Israelites cried out to the Lord, He always raised up a deliverer.

This pattern is often repeated in our lives. We make mistakes, fail to notice the enemy creeping in, let our prayer lives get slack, or even engage in sinful behaviors and find ourselves in a miserable condition. But when we cry out, God will deliver us. It may take time to work out all the circumstances we got ourselves into, but the sound of now in our cries will cause God to come running.

Psalm 145:19 tells us that "He will fulfill the desire of those who fear Him; He also will hear their cry and save them." He hears your cries for breakthrough in the situation that is trying to break you. David knew this, which is why he often prayed along these lines: "Hear my cry, O God; attend to my prayer" (Psalm 61:1). And again: "Hear a just cause, O LORD, attend to my cry; give ear to my prayer which is not from deceitful lips" (Psalm 17:1).

Father Will Move Heaven and Earth

David gives a dramatic account of a desperate situation in which he found himself, and how God moved. Second Samuel 22:6–20 offers a picture of a good, good Father who hears the cry—the loud sound, the call (with the name of God), and the desperate summoning—for help.

Hear this as if God is doing this for you, because God is no respecter of persons. What He did for David, He is ready, willing and able to do for you, too—but you have to release the sound of now that demonstrates your urgent desperation and faith in the God who can move heaven and earth for His children.

Read this dramatic passage: "The sorrows of Sheol surrounded me; the snares of death confronted me. In my distress I called upon the LORD, and cried out to my God; He heard my voice from His temple, and my cry entered His ears" (2 Samuel 22:6–7).

Now imagine this scene. *The Message* translates it this way:

> The waves of death crashed over me, devil waters rushed over me. Hell's ropes cinched me tight; death traps barred every exit. A hostile world! I called to GOD, to my God I cried out. From his palace he heard me call; my cry brought me right into his presence—a private audience!

I like this translation because it conveys David's desperation. When you feel as though the waves of death are crashing over you and the devil's waters are rushing against you and hell's ropes are holding you, you will either lie down and die or release the sound of now—and God will respond. Watch how God moves in response to David's cry—his sound of now:

"Then the earth shook and trembled; the foundations of heaven quaked and were shaken, because He was angry. Smoke went up from His nostrils, and devouring fire from His mouth; coals were kindled by it. He bowed the heavens also, and came down with darkness under His feet. He rode upon a cherub, and flew; and He was seen upon the wings of the wind. He made darkness canopies around Him, dark waters and thick clouds of the skies. From the brightness before Him coals of fire were kindled."

2 Samuel 22:8–13

This is like a momma bear going after someone who messes with her cub! (Actually, it is far more intense, but you get the idea.) I know that when people messed with my daughter, I rose up to move heaven and earth to defend her. My motto was, "You can mess with me, but you can't mess with her!" When the enemy comes against you, God does not just sit idly by and observe. He is watching and listening actively for you to cry out with the sound of now. He wants to come to your rescue. The passage continues:

"The LORD thundered from heaven, and the Most High uttered His voice. He sent out arrows and scattered them; lightning bolts, and He vanquished them. Then the channels of the sea were seen, the foundations of the world were uncovered, at the rebuke of the LORD, at the blast of the breath of His nostrils.

"He sent from above, He took me, He drew me out of many waters. He delivered me from my strong enemy, from those who hated me; for they were too strong for me. They confronted me in the day of my calamity, but the LORD was my support. He also brought me out into a broad place; He delivered me because He delighted in me."

2 Samuel 22:14–20

Meditate on that. God delivered David from his "strong enemy" after he released the sound of now. David's enemies were too strong for him, but they were not too strong for his God. David knew this and cried out accordingly. God responded by delivering him, putting him in a broad place because He delighted in David. God delights in you, too!

6

The Sound of Now Unlocks Wisdom and Revelation

Wisdom and revelation usually come before my break-throughs. I have an aha moment—a sudden wisdom nugget drops into my lap or a missing revelation enlightens my spirit so I know what to do and how to do it. At times, wisdom and revelation guide me toward a spiritual warfare strategy. Other times, wisdom and revelation lead me to repentance. Still other times, wisdom and revelation inspire me to connect with someone who holds a key.

When I look back, I realize that the wisdom and revelation that preceded my breakthroughs always came in response to the sound of now. They might have come as a prophetic word, a dream, a vision, a Scripture, a divine appointment or some other way, but they came after I released a certain sound in prayer. It was a desperate prayer from a humble heart that knows "I don't know what I don't know"—but I can ask the One who does know.

Some years ago I needed a financial breakthrough in the ministry. There was no lack, but I was prophetically sensing a shift in my assignments and wanted to position myself for sustained breakthrough. At the time, I had no idea God would soon lead me to resign as editor of *Charisma* magazine to move into full-time ministry. Of course, God knew, and He was leading me to pray for wisdom and revelation in the area of finances.

I needed to know where He wanted me to sow. While you already reap more than you sow according to the law of the harvest, it matters where you sow. God has a harvest in mind, and in order to unlock that harvest, you need to sow in the right field. As I do every year, I prayed for wisdom and revelation about my giving strategy—where to give, how much to give, whether to shift my giving to another ministry and so on. Soon, I had a dream.

In the dream, I was driving a well-known prophet to the airport. We stopped on the way to get something to eat, but we had to hurry because the restaurant was closing. I was working to handle all the details and make the entire journey as smooth as possible.

She asked me, "Why are you doing all this for me?" She knew that I had no time to spare to run to the airport, considering my already overloaded schedule at *Charisma*, along with writing books and traveling in ministry.

I responded, "I'm sowing."

This dream was from the Lord. I never told this prophet about it. But over the years, I have sown large amounts into this prophet's ministry and have seen breakthrough after breakthrough after breakthrough in my life. I have seen ministry breakthrough, personal breakthrough, financial breakthrough and more. What unlocked that wisdom and revelation? The sound of effective fervent prayers from a meek spirit that fears God. Indeed, the Bible speaks of "sound" wisdom, but there is also a sound that unlocks wisdom—and revelation—leading to breakthrough.

Solomon's Prayer for Wisdom

The Bible gives us a precedent for the sound that unlocks wisdom and revelation in Solomon's story, which, incidentally, also involves a dream. David's son Solomon was not the heir apparent to the throne by birthright, and he was only twenty years old when he was crowned king. Although David gave Solomon instructions before he died, the young king would soon realize that leading a nation—especially in the shadow of his beloved warrior-king father—was a daunting task.

While Solomon was offering sacrifices at Gibeon, the Lord showed up one night in a dream and asked him a question: "Ask! What shall I give you?" (1 Kings 3:5) We read Solomon's response in verses 6–9:

> And Solomon said: "You have shown great mercy to Your servant David my father, because he walked before You in truth, in righteousness, and in uprightness of heart with You; You have continued this great kindness for him, and You have given him a son to sit on his throne, as it is this day. Now, O LORD my God, You have made Your servant king instead of my father David, but I am a little child; I do not know how to go out or come in. And Your servant is in the midst of Your people whom You have chosen, a great people, too numerous to be numbered or counted. Therefore give to Your servant an understanding heart to judge Your people, that I may discern between good and evil. For who is able to judge this great people of Yours?"

Let's stop there and notice a few elements of Solomon's posture in prayer that released the sound of now. Keep in mind: Solomon needed a breakthrough in wisdom *in that immediate moment*. He was a young king facing many challenges *in that immediate moment*. He was desperate for wisdom *in that immediate moment*. Solomon did not just pray fervently; he prayed with humility and in the fear of the Lord. Solomon acknowledged who God is, his own weakness and his dependence on God to help him lead His people. Then he made his petition for wisdom.

Can you see it? Inspired by the Holy Spirit, Solomon would later write, "In all your ways acknowledge Him, and He shall direct your paths" (Proverbs 3:6). And, "The fear of the LORD is the beginning of wisdom, and the knowledge of the Holy One is understanding" (Proverbs 9:10). In fact, Solomon received a tremendous revelation of the fear of the Lord and humility, which he displayed throughout the books of Proverbs and Ecclesiastes.

Look how the Lord responded to the sound of now that Solomon released in humility and reverence, as recorded in 1 Kings 3:10–15:

> The speech pleased the Lord, that Solomon had asked this thing. Then God said to him: "Because you have asked this thing, and have not asked long life for yourself, nor have asked riches for yourself, nor have asked the life of your enemies, but have asked for yourself understanding to discern justice, behold, I have done according to your words; see, I have given you a wise and understanding heart, so that there has not been anyone like you before you, nor shall any like you arise after you. And I have also given you what you have not asked: both riches and honor, so that there shall not be anyone like you among the kings all your days. So if you walk

in My ways, to keep My statutes and My commandments, as your father David walked, then I will lengthen your days."

Then Solomon awoke; and indeed it had been a dream.

The sound of now does not work when we release it with a demanding spirit. The sound of now does not work when we want to fuel personal ambition. The sound of now that releases wisdom and revelation unto breakthrough seeks the Lord's direction with a heart that is desperate, humble and reverent. What was the result of Solomon's sound? Breakthrough after breakthrough after breakthrough. Solomon was the richest man on the face of the earth, and all his enemies were at peace with him as long as he walked in humble reverence before the Lord.

It Is Wisdom to Pray for Wisdom

Wisdom is one of my chief prayer requests. Although I pray for all sorts of things and my prayer focus shifts based on specific needs, wisdom is a staple of my prayer life. I have learned that if I pray for wisdom and revelation from a humble heart that acknowledges God as the wise ruler of the universe, then I will fare well in every area of life most of the time. In fact, if I had to choose between praying for more wisdom or more money, I would pray for more wisdom every time. When you have wisdom, many other things fall into place.

As I mentioned in chapter 3, James, the apostle of practical faith, penned these Spirit-inspired words: "If any of you lacks wisdom, let him ask of God, who gives to all liberally and without reproach, and it will be given to him" (James 1:5). Notice the verse speaks to *anyone*. That includes you.

63

No matter what you did to get yourself into a mess, God will give you wisdom and revelation to get out of it if you ask with a humble, reverent heart—and in faith. Indeed, God is no respecter of persons (see Acts 10:34).

Solomon walked in wisdom and in breakthrough. Look how he described the fruit of this manner of prayer. He speaks about a breakthrough lifestyle from experience in Proverbs 3:13–18 (TPT):

> Those who find true wisdom obtain the tools for understanding, the proper way to live, for they will have a fountain of blessing pouring into their lives. To gain the riches of wisdom is far greater than gaining the wealth of the world. As wisdom increases, a great treasure is imparted, greater than many bars of refined gold. It is a more valuable commodity than gold and gemstones, for there is nothing you desire that could compare to her. Wisdom extends to you long life in one hand and wealth and promotion in the other. Out of her mouth flows righteousness, and her words release both law and mercy. The ways of wisdom are sweet, always drawing you into the place of wholeness. Seeking for her brings the discovery of untold blessings, for she is the healing tree of life to those who taste her fruits.

Wisdom will keep and guard you if you love it (see Proverbs 4:6–7). By wisdom your house is built (see Proverbs 24:3). A man's wisdom makes his face shine (see Ecclesiastes 8:1). The ear of the wise seeks knowledge (see Proverbs 18:15). The wise man listens to advice (see Proverbs 12:15). Wise ones are cautious and turn away from evil (see Proverbs 14:16). The words of the wise win him favor (see Ecclesiastes 10:12). The wise will inherit honor (see Proverbs 3:35). Study for yourself what the Bible says about wisdom, then pray for it with a humble, reverent heart and watch wisdom and revelation for breakthrough come.

Also pray Paul's apostolic prayer in Ephesians:

> That the God of our Lord Jesus Christ, the Father of glory, may give to you the spirit of wisdom and revelation in the knowledge of Him, the eyes of your understanding being enlightened; that you may know what is the hope of His calling, what are the riches of the glory of His inheritance in the saints, and what is the exceeding greatness of His power toward us who believe, according to the working of His mighty power which He worked in Christ when He raised Him from the dead and seated Him at His right hand in the heavenly places, far above all principality and power and might and dominion, and every name that is named, not only in this age but also in that which is to come.
>
> Ephesians 1:17–21

Receiving Breakthrough Revelation

We need wisdom and revelation in the knowledge of Christ, wisdom and revelation for the affairs of life, wisdom and revelation—and understanding—for our times and seasons so we can do the will of God in His timing. This is the bedrock of many miracle breakthroughs.

It seems Solomon learned from his father, David, who asked for revelation over and over again. David asked the Lord if the men of Keilah would deliver him into the hand of Saul—and the Lord confirmed they would (see 1 Samuel 23:10–12). David's revelation allowed him and his six hundred men to escape. David needed the revelation now. He released the sound of now and got a now revelation that led to a life-saving breakthrough.

David had a habit of asking the Lord if he should go up to certain places. In 2 Samuel 2:1–4, we read another inquiry David made of the Lord:

> "Shall I go up to any of the cities of Judah?"
> And the LORD said to him, "Go up."
> David said, "Where shall I go up?"
> And He said, "To Hebron."
> So David went up there, and his two wives also, Ahinoam the Jezreelitess, and Abigail the widow of Nabal the Carmelite. And David brought up the men who were with him, every man with his household. So they dwelt in the cities of Hebron.
> Then the men of Judah came, and there they anointed David king over the house of Judah.

David got his breakthrough into kingship by following the revelation of the Lord. David had waited decades for the prophetic word from Samuel to come to pass. He hid from Saul for years waiting to be crowned king. Even after Saul's death, David did not presume to demand the crown. He asked the Lord, "Shall I go up?"

See, the sound of now does not work if it comes from a selfish heart. The breakthrough comes when we are sold out to God's will and release a desperate sound to bring His will to the earth.

David asked the Lord for revelation in the face of a horrifying situation in which the Amalekites had plundered his camp at Ziklag and captured the women and children of his armed forces: "So David inquired of the LORD, saying, 'Shall I pursue this troop? Shall I overtake them?' And He answered him, 'Pursue, for you shall surely overtake them and without fail recover all'" (1 Samuel 30:8).

This was David's usual practice. With the enemy Philistines, for example, it might have been Samson's style to pick fights in order to get breakthrough, but humble David began by seeking a revelation from the Lord. In one example, found in 2 Samuel 5:19, we read: "David inquired of the LORD, saying, 'Shall I go up against the Philistines? Will You deliver them into my hand?' And the LORD said to David, 'Go up, for I will doubtless deliver the Philistines into your hand.'"

Reasoning or Revelation?

Gideon asked for revelation over and over again, albeit in the form of a fleece. I do not believe we should put out fleeces—asking God for signs as a primary way of revelation—because we have the Holy Spirit who promises to show us things to come (see John 16:13). But Gideon did not have the Holy Spirit when God told him to save Israel from the hand of the Midianites. He sought revelation the only way he knew how (see Judges 6).

One reason I do not like fleeces is because we can reason ourselves into false revelation or out of true revelation. We have the God-given ability to reason. Each of us is spirit, soul and body. The soul comprises the mind, will and emotions. Our minds contain our intellect, imagination and reasoning. When we are desperate for a breakthrough we can reason ourselves into confusion over what to do and how to do it. It is okay to reason things out, to a degree, but we have to be careful to submit our reasoning to the Lord because our hearts are deceitful above all things (see Jeremiah 17:9) and knowledge puffs us up (see 1 Corinthians 8:1).

Remember, the sound of now that unlocks wisdom and revelation is based on desperation, humility and the fear of the Lord—for pride comes before destruction (see Proverbs 16:18). If we rely on our human reasoning alone, we can talk ourselves out of the wisdom and revelation that lead us to the breakthrough. We see this play out in the life of Peter, the fisherman turned disciple turned apostle.

Imagine the scene. Jesus stood by the Lake of Gennesaret with the multitudes pressing in. He got into Peter's boat and asked him to put out a little from the shore. After He finished preaching, Jesus turned to Peter and gave him a prophetic revelation that promised massive breakthrough where there had only been disappointment:

> "Launch out into the deep and let down your nets for a catch."
>
> But Simon answered and said to Him, "Master, we have toiled all night and caught nothing; nevertheless at Your word I will let down the net." And when they had done this, they caught a great number of fish, and their net was breaking. So they signaled to their partners in the other boat to come and help them. And they came and filled both the boats, so that they began to sink.
>
> Luke 5:4–7

The revelation did not meet with Peter's natural knowledge and reasoning. Some people would have been so full of pride in their skill that they would have talked themselves out of their miracle breakthrough.

Thankfully, God does not give up on us when we miss it. We can try again. He wants us to get the breakthrough, but we have to do it His way.

7

Discerning the Sound of War

I felt a rumbling in the spirit. I knew something was about to happen. It was not like the rumbling of an earthquake (see Hebrews 12:18–19). It was not like the rumbling of thunder in a rainstorm (see Job 38:25). It was not like the rumbling of God's voice (see Job 37:2). I could not completely discern it at first, but it was a definite rumble in the spirit.

After I had prayed and pondered this sound, the Holy Spirit quickened to me the memory of a prophetic word I had released several months earlier about things coming to a head. As I pressed into the Spirit, I realized it was the symbolic rumble of Jehu's chariot. It was like the sound of Jehu riding to throw down Jezebel. By the word of the Lord to Elijah, Jehu was anointed to throw Jezebel down and immediately starting driving his chariot furiously (see 1 Kings 19:16; 2 Kings 9:1–10, 20). In plain English, he was driving with righteous indignation like a man on a mission. It was the sound of war.

Jehu was not on a covert operation. His chariot was rumbling as the horses ran at full speed to complete his God-given assignment, slaying everyone in his path who would not join his cause. Queen Jezebel herself was in bondage to evil; according to Revelation 2:20, her name also represents a seducing spirit that leads people away from Jesus to serve idols and commit sexual immorality.[1]

From hand-to-hand combat with swords and the rumbling of iron chariots in Jehu's Old Testament times to muskets and canons in the American Revolutionary War to air strikes in World War I to nuclear bombs in World War II to secret cyber wars in the twenty-first century, the sound of war in the earthly realm has changed over the past three thousand years. But the sound of war in the spirit remains constant. We have to discern it and release the right sound in response.

Broadening our Jehu example to the spiritual realm, we find that principalities like Jezebel release powers, such as the weapon of witchcraft, against us. Witchcraft is the power of the enemy, a counterfeit to the power of God the Holy Spirit. In order to walk in breakthrough, we have to discern the sound of war and the sound of the weapons the enemy is releasing so we can release the right sound—the right word—to combat them. Keep in mind that different weapons make different sounds. The sound of fear is different from the sound of rejection. Demons have voices, and they combat our minds with vain imaginations (see 2 Corinthians 10:4–5; Romans 1:21).

Make no mistake: There is a war for your breakthrough. The enemy comes to steal, kill and destroy—and he makes a sound while he is doing it. First Peter 5:8 tells us that the enemy roams about like a roaring lion seeking someone to devour. Just as we need to tune our ears to the sound of God, we need to understand the sound of a lurking enemy so we can respond appropriately. You cannot hear it with your natural ears, but if you tune your ears to the spiritual realm, you can hear it and go on the offense.

David made a deadly mistake that brought deadly consequences into his generations: He did not discern the sound of war. In fact, David was on the rooftop instead of on the battlefield during a season when kings go to war (see 2 Samuel 11:1–2). He watched a woman named Bathsheba bathe, had intimate relations with her, had her husband murdered to cover up the sin, lost the newborn child, saw his daughter Tamar raped by one of his sons, experienced the pain of his son Absalom taking revenge on his brother, then usurping David's authority and taking the kingdom. And the consequences go on and on.

If David had discerned the sound of war, he would have reigned victorious in battle. (David never lost a battle.) Instead of a breakthrough, he let the enemy in to break down his family relations and damage his relationship with God.

Discerning the Mind Battle

The sound of war often hits your mind first in the form of vain imaginations—subtle suggestions or all-out lies from the enemy. The enemy's suggestions may sound like your own thoughts because he often uses the first person—"I am depressed . . . I am afraid." Other times the sound of the enemy's vain imaginations might sound like God's Word.

Satan tried to fool Jesus with this line:

"If You are the Son of God, throw Yourself down. For it is written: 'He shall give His angels charge over you,' and, 'in their hands they shall bear you up, lest you dash your foot

71

against a stone.'" Jesus said to him, "It is written again, 'You shall not tempt the LORD your God.'"

Matthew 4:6–7

Jesus did not fall for the mind tricks because He knew the Word (you could say, He knew Himself). The enemy tries to take God's Word out of context so we will misstep and fall into his trap.

How do you discern the battle against your mind? The Bible says that Satan was more subtle, or crafty, than any other creature in the Garden (see Genesis 3:1). Many times, we never discern that our minds are under demonic attack because of the enemy's subtle nature. Consider these seven signs that the battle in your mind is raging:

1. Your mind is racing with fear, worry, depression, anger or other unhealthy thoughts.

I call this the "mind-traffic train." I heard the Lord say this:

> Do not fret; do not worry because it only leads to evil. Stop thinking what could happen. Stop thinking about what the enemy wants to tell you, but begin to think about what I've told you can happen—what I've told you is possible, because all things are possible to those who believe. And this mind traffic that comes to steal your joy— you've got to release it. You've got to refuse to accept it. You've got to stop dwelling on things that you could do nothing about, and realize that I am a God of "all things are possible." I am the God of reconciliation. I am the God of provision and restitution. I am the God who has your back. So

remember, when the mind traffic comes, turn it all around. Turn your thoughts toward the opposite direction; purposely think opposite of what the mind traffic is trying to tell you.

2. You experience feelings of being overwhelmed.

Overwhelmingness is not from God. When over-whelmingness knocks at the door of your soul, keep your focus on God. Take a page out of David's play-book in Psalm 142:

> I cry out to the LORD with my voice; with my voice to the LORD I make my supplication. I pour out my complaint before Him; I declare before Him my trouble.
>
> When my spirit was overwhelmed within me, then You knew my path. In the way in which I walk they have secretly set a snare for me. Look on my right hand and see, for there is no one who acknowledges me; refuge has failed me; no one cares for my soul.
>
> I cried out to You, O LORD: I said, "You are my refuge, my portion in the land of the living. Attend to my cry, for I am brought very low; deliver me from my persecutors, for they are stronger than I. Bring my soul out of prison, that I may praise Your name; the righteous shall surround me, for You shall deal bountifully with me."

3. You are tempted to return to unhealthy habits or sinful lifestyles.

One of the enemy's names in Scripture is "tempter." He wants to kick you when you are down so he can come in for the kill. He knows the wages of sin is death (see Romans 6:23).

4. You isolate yourself from others.

Isolation is a demonic strategy to separate you from the Body of Christ so the enemy can back you into a corner and leave you without help. Hebrews 10:25 (TPT) tells us,

> This is not the time to pull away and neglect meeting together, as some have formed the habit of doing, because we need each other! In fact, we should come together even more frequently, eager to encourage and urge each other onward as we anticipate that day dawning.

5. You do not want to—or you simply cannot—read the Word, spend time with God or pray.

Many times the power of witchcraft makes it nearly impossible to stay focused. Your mind wanders. You feel like falling asleep when you set out to do spiritual things. This is a sign that your mind is under siege. The enemy wants to dry you up and dry you out so you will wither spiritually.

6. Your emotions are going haywire.

You can discern the battle against your mind—wrong thoughts—by paying attention to your emotions. Wrong thoughts spur wrong feelings. Feelings of strong confusion about your life, who you are, what you should do, feelings like condemnation or other strong emotions that seem to manifest for no specific reason can point to warfare against your mind.

Paul made it crystal clear in his Spirit-inspired words in 1 Corinthians 14:33: "God is not the author of confusion but of peace." Although this is true in any context, it is telling that Paul spoke these words in relation to prophecy. Look at the passage in its entirety:

> For you can all prophesy one by one, that all may learn and all may be encouraged. And the spirits of the prophets are subject to the prophets. For God is not the author of confusion but of peace, as in all the churches of the saints.
>
> 1 Corinthians 14:31–33

When feelings of confusion hit your mind—when you cannot seem to put your mind in order—stop and trace your thoughts. It is likely demons are prophesying to you. The Bible labels the devil's prophesied lies *vain imaginations*. Second Corinthians 10:5 tells us what to do with these intruders: Cast them down.

7. You want to give up.

When you feel discouraged, distressed, depressed, ready to throw in the towel and call it quits, you can be sure the Spirit of God is not leading you. God always leads us into triumph through Christ Jesus (see 2 Corinthians 2:14). The enemy wants you to take your hand off the plow God has assigned you and walk away. God never gives up on you and will not lead you to give up in a discouraged, distressed, depressed state. When He calls you out of something, it is because He is calling you into something else. You will transition with a ring of victory, not a drumbeat of defeat.

When Peace Leaves

Sometimes the sound of war is a disturbance of peace. You have to understand the sound of peace in order to discern the sound of war. When Jehu was on the way to throw down Queen Jezebel, he was confronted by Joram, reigning son of King Ahab.

Joram called out, "Is it peace, Jehu?"

Jehu answered, "What peace, as long as the harlotries of your mother Jezebel and her witchcraft are so many?" (2 Kings 9:22). In times of war, you can have peace in your spirit, but there can be a disruption in your soul or the spiritual atmosphere.

Sixteenth-century priest St. Ignatius of Loyola once said:

If in the course of the thoughts . . . it ends in something bad, of a distracting tendency, or less good than what the soul had previously proposed to do, or if it weakens it or disquiets or disturbs the soul, taking away its peace, tranquility and quiet, which it had before, it is a clear sign that it proceeds from the evil spirit, enemy of our profit and eternal salvation.[2]

What does peace sound like? Paul the apostle wrote:

Whatever things are true, whatever things are noble, whatever things are just, whatever things are pure, whatever things are lovely, whatever things are of good report, if there is any virtue and if there is anything praiseworthy—meditate on these things. The things which you learned and received and heard and saw in me, these do, and the God of peace will be with you.

Philippians 4:8–9

When you learn how to walk in peace—when you operate in the peace of God that surpasses all understanding, that guards your heart and mind in Christ Jesus—you will discern the sound of war. After all, the Kingdom of God is righteousness, peace and joy in the Holy Spirit (see Romans 14:17).

8

The Sound of Now Sends Confusion into the Enemy's Camp

Many intercessors love to pray these words: "I release confusion into the enemy's camp." I have done that many times myself at Awakening House of Prayer. But technically, we are not the ones releasing the confusion—God is. That might mess with your theology because we know that God is not the author of confusion but of peace (see 1 Corinthians 14:33). He can, however, and does send confusion into the enemy's camp to fulfill His purposes—and this is often in response to the sound of now through praise and imprecatory prayers that implore the God of all justice to do the impossible.

Cry Out to God

Jehoshaphat was facing an impossible battle. Second Chronicles 20 records his predicament: The Moabites, the Ammonites and other unidentified "ites" were arranging themselves in battle against him. Indeed, people were running to the king in a frenzy to report that a "great multitude is coming against you from beyond the sea" (verse 2). Jehoshaphat's first response was fear, but he shook off fear to seek the Lord. The king proclaimed a fast throughout all Judah, then he released the sound of now, crying out to God in a desperate prayer as the enemy was moving in like a flood.

> "O LORD God of our fathers, are You not God in heaven, and do You not rule over all the kingdoms of the nations, and in Your hand is there not power and might, so that no one is able to withstand You? Are You not our God, who drove out the inhabitants of this land before Your people Israel, and gave it to the descendants of Abraham Your friend forever?
>
> "And they dwell in it, and have built You a sanctuary in it for Your name, saying, 'If disaster comes upon us—sword, judgment, pestilence, or famine—we will stand before this temple and in Your presence (for Your name is in this temple), and cry out to You in our affliction, and You will hear and save.'
>
> "And now, here are the people of Ammon, Moab, and Mount Seir—whom You would not let Israel invade when they came out of the land of Egypt, but they turned from them and did not destroy them—here they are, rewarding us by coming to throw us out of Your possession which You have given us to inherit. O our God, will You not judge them? For we have no power against this great multitude that is coming against us; nor do we know what to do, but our eyes are upon You."
>
> 2 Chronicles 20:6–12

Praise Him in Advance

The sound of now not only captured God's attention but also caused Him to take the battle into His own hands. Jehoshaphat released this desperate sound of faith by acknowledging God's power, might and the Abrahamic covenant. He appealed to God's justice and mercy and Israel's helplessness against the great multitude. Finally, Jehoshaphat determined to keep his eyes on God despite impossible odds of winning the war.

That sound of now unlocked a prophetic warfare strategy. Jahaziel prophesied,

> "Listen, all you of Judah and you inhabitants of Jerusalem, and you, King Jehoshaphat! Thus says the LORD to you: 'Do not be afraid nor dismayed because of this great multitude, for the battle is not yours, but God's. Tomorrow go down against them. They will surely come up by the Ascent of Ziz, and you will find them at the end of the brook before the Wilderness of Jeruel. You will not need to fight in this battle. Position yourselves, stand still and see the salvation of the LORD, who is with you, O Judah and Jerusalem!' Do not fear or be dismayed; tomorrow go out against them, for the LORD is with you."
>
> 2 Chronicles 20:15–17

Judah's response? The people released the sound of worship to the Lord. They praised Him with voices loud and high.

The next morning, they went out to the battlefield. King Jehoshaphat encouraged Judah to believe the prophetic word and act on it. What happened next demonstrates a miracle breakthrough through the sound of now in praise and worship:

> [Jehoshaphat] explained his plan and appointed men to march in front of the army and praise the LORD for his holy power by singing: "Praise the LORD! His love never ends." As soon as they began singing, the LORD confused the enemy camp, so that the Ammonite and Moabite troops attacked

and completely destroyed those from Edom. Then they turned against each other and fought until the entire camp was wiped out!

2 Chronicles 20:21–23 CEV

Look what happened! The children of Israel did not even have to sing and praise for hours and hours. The key here was not to praise and worship in the unfortunate way that many do in Sunday service—distracted by their neighbors, thinking about lunch or waiting for worship to end so they can hear the Word. Through their faith-inspired praise and worship, the army released the sound of now, and it worked immediately and thoroughly. There was no living enemy to battle after the Lord sent confusion into the enemy's camp.

The story continues in 2 Chronicles 20:24–25 (CEV):

When Judah's army reached the tower that overlooked the desert, they saw that every soldier in the enemy's army was lying dead on the ground. So Jehoshaphat and his troops went into the camp to carry away everything of value. They found a large herd of livestock, a lot of equipment, clothes, and other valuable things. It took them three days to carry it all away, and there was still some left over.

By releasing the sound of now through wholehearted praise and worship, not only did they escape what appeared to be certain death, but they also carried away the spoils of a war they did not fight. What a breakthrough! Verses 26–30 (CEV) offer the end of the story, which is important to read:

Then on the fourth day, everyone came together in Beracah Valley and sang praises to the LORD. That's why that place was called Praise Valley.

Jehoshaphat led the crowd back to Jerusalem. And as they marched, they played harps and blew trumpets. They were very happy because the LORD had given them victory over their enemies, so when they reached the city, they went straight to the temple.

When the other nations heard how the LORD had fought against Judah's enemies, they were too afraid to invade Judah. The LORD let Jehoshaphat's kingdom be at peace.

Notice two additional results of the sound of now. The lesson of praising Him was so profound they actually called the area Praise Valley as a memorial and kept on praising after the battle was over. Some of us praise God in advance but we forget to say, "Thank You, Jesus," after the victory. Jehoshaphat and Judah were overwhelmed by the breakthrough.

Secondly, because the slaughter was so great, the sound of now led Jehoshaphat's kingdom into peace. Their enemies were too afraid to engage in battle with God's people.

God Confirms This Strategy

There are a number of biblical examples of this strategy of crying out to God, and His response of releasing confusion into the enemy's camp. Look at 1 Samuel 7:7–12:

> Now when the Philistines heard that the children of Israel had gathered together at Mizpah, the lords of the Philistines went up against Israel. And when the children of Israel heard of it, they were afraid of the Philistines. So the children of Israel said to Samuel, "Do not cease to cry out to the LORD our God for us, that He may save us from the hand of the Philistines."

And Samuel took a suckling lamb and offered it as a whole burnt offering to the LORD. Then Samuel cried out to the LORD for Israel, and the LORD answered him. Now as Samuel was offering up the burnt offering, the Philistines drew near to battle against Israel. But the LORD thundered with a loud thunder upon the Philistines that day, and so confused them that they were overcome before Israel. And the men of Israel went out of Mizpah and pursued the Philistines, and drove them back as far as below Beth Car. Then Samuel took a stone and set it up between Mizpah and Shen, and called its name Ebenezer, saying, "Thus far the LORD has helped us."

God offered a repeat performance in 1 Samuel 14:19–21:

Now it happened, while Saul talked to the priest, that the noise which was in the camp of the Philistines continued to increase; so Saul said to the priest, "Withdraw your hand." Then Saul and all the people who were with him assembled, and they went to the battle; and indeed every man's sword was against his neighbor, and there was very great confusion. Moreover the Hebrews who were with the Philistines before that time, who went up with them into the camp from the surrounding country, they also joined the Israelites who were with Saul and Jonathan.

In Exodus 23:27, God promises His people, "I will send My fear before you, I will cause confusion among all the people to whom you come, and will make all your enemies turn their backs to you."

God responds to our cries. The sound of now causes Him to break in and release confusion against the enemies that are working to confound us.

Issuing Imprecatory Prayers

Imprecatory prayers can also cause God to release confusion into the enemy's camp. Some call imprecatory prayers cursing prayers, but biblical imprecatory prayers are simply asking God to release judgment on enemies in the spirit. Again, we are not praying imprecatory prayers against people—but spirits. Most of the imprecatory prayers in the Bible are found in the book of Psalms.

For example, in Psalm 70:1–3, David prayed,

> Make haste, O God, to deliver me; make haste to help me, O Lord! Let them be ashamed and confounded who seek my life; let them be turned back and confused who desire my hurt. Let them be turned back because of their shame, who say, "Aha, aha!"

And in Psalm 35:1–8, he cried out,

> Plead my cause, O Lord, with those who strive with me; fight against those who fight against me. Take hold of shield and buckler, and stand up for my help. Also draw out the spear, and stop those who pursue me. Say to my soul, "I am your salvation."
>
> Let those be put to shame and brought to dishonor who seek after my life; Let those be turned back and brought to confusion who plot my hurt. Let them be like chaff before the wind, and let the angel of the Lord chase them. Let their way be dark and slippery, and let the angel of the Lord pursue them.
>
> For without cause they have hidden their net for me in a pit, which they have dug without cause for my life. Let destruction come upon him unexpectedly, and let his net that he has hidden catch himself; into that very destruction let him fall.

Imprecatory prayer should not be your first line of offense (or defense). As with any other manifestation of the sound of now, you should be Spirit-inspired. Imprecatory prayers are generally reserved for situations where you require justice against your enemies, where principalities may be at hand and you need God and His warring angels to fight them on your behalf. This type of prayer is also effective against stubborn demons. An imprecatory prayer is like a nuclear bomb.

9

The Sound of Now Breaks Down Barriers to Your Promised Land

It was enough. The spirit of betrayal was taking out my staff. False prophets were rising up against me to curse me. All of us involved in this ministry were taking hits left and right. The onslaught was relentless. It did not seem as if our spiritual warfare prayers were accomplishing anything. Of course, we knew that was not true, but that is what it looked like. (Imagine if we had not been praying effective, fervent prayers!)

When Christian International Ministries founder Bishop Bill Hamon, my spiritual father, came to speak at our annual Ascend conference, I told him about the issues and how we were fighting but seeing no lasting breakthrough.

Without hesitation he told me, "We're going to shut all this down." And we did. We shut it down with the sound of now combined with prophetic acts.

A full explanation of Bishop Hamon's teaching on this point is given in his book *God's Weapons of War* (Chosen, 2018). In essence, the sound of now can manifest through the shout of faith—and it did. I saw demons pushing each other in order to get out of the way. When the shout of faith goes up, the walls must come down.

When we shout in a time of war, we are following the example of our God. After all, He is the God who shouts. Psalm 47:5 tells us, "God has gone up with a shout." Isaiah 42:13 tells us, "The LORD shall go forth like a mighty man; He shall stir up His zeal like a man of war. He shall cry out, yes, shout aloud; He shall prevail against His enemies." And Amos 1:14 reveals that God "will kindle a fire in the wall of Rabbah, and it shall devour its palaces, amid shouting in the day of battle, and a tempest in the day of the whirlwind."

Releasing Your Battle Cry

The very definition of *shout* is "to utter in a loud voice." The Hebrew word for *shout*—*tsarach*—has several definitions, including "to roar, to make a shrill or clear sound, and to cry out as in a battle cry," according to *The KJV Hebrew Old Testament Lexicon*.[1] This is a different kind of crying out from that which Bartimaeus released. This is an aggressive, militant war cry.

Although the Israelites shook with fear in silence when Goliath made the challenge for one of their soldiers to go toe-to-toe with him in battle, they made a different noise after David had defeated the giant. When the Israelites heard the sound of Goliath's body hitting the ground and the Philistine army fleeing, they released a battle cry:

> Now the men of Israel and Judah arose and shouted, and pursued the Philistines as far as the entrance of the valley and to the gates of Ekron. And the wounded of the Philistines

fell along the road to Shaaraim, even as far as Gath and Ekron. Then the children of Israel returned from chasing the Philistines, and they plundered their tents.

1 Samuel 17:52–53

The shout sent a message to the Philistines that the Israelites would not be their servants as the giant had prophesied, and it galvanized the warriors to unite against a common enemy. I imagine the Philistines never forgot that day—or the sound of an emboldened Israeli army pursuing them.

The Right Time to Shout

God is patient if we need His assurance before shouting out a war cry. More than a century before David killed the giant, Gideon led a small army into what also looked like an impossible task.

The Lord had charged Gideon with delivering Israel from the hands of the oppressive Midianites. As we noted earlier, Gideon could hardly believe it, so he put out two wool fleeces to make sure it was really the Lord, and became a reluctant captain of the Lord's earthly army. God winnowed out all the Israelites who were fearful, and Gideon was left with just three hundred soldiers. God did not want men taking His glory (see Judges 7:2).

Despite all of the supernatural signs and prophetic communication, Gideon was still a bit nervous at the prospect of going out against Israel's oppressors who outnumbered them by masses. God, in His mercy, gave Gideon one more prophetic sign.

Gideon overheard a Midianite telling his friend about a dream he had had the night before. In the dream, a loaf of barley bread tumbled into the Midianite camp and struck a tent. The tent collapsed. His friend interpreted the dream this way: "This is nothing else but the sword of Gideon the son of Joash, a man of Israel! Into his hand God has delivered Midian and the whole camp" (Judges 7:14).

With this, Gideon was emboldened and addressed his mini army. We see what happens next in Judges 7:15–20 (NLT):

> When Gideon heard the dream and its interpretation, he bowed in worship before the LORD. Then he returned to the Israelite camp and shouted, "Get up! For the LORD has given you victory over the Midianite hordes!" He divided the 300 men into three groups and gave each man a ram's horn and a clay jar with a torch in it.
>
> Then he said to them, "Keep your eyes on me. When I come to the edge of the camp, do just as I do. As soon as I and those with me blow the rams' horns, blow your horns, too, all around the entire camp, and shout, 'For the LORD and for Gideon!'"
>
> It was just after midnight, after the changing of the guard, when Gideon and the 100 men with him reached the edge of the Midianite camp. Suddenly, they blew the rams' horns and broke their clay jars. Then all three groups blew their horns and broke their jars. They held the blazing torches in their left hands and the horns in their right hands, and they all shouted, "A sword for the LORD and for Gideon!"

Gideon released his war cry, which caused the Midianites to "[rush] around in a panic, shouting as they ran to escape" (verse 21). The shout and the blowing of the rams' horns caused the Midianite warriors to fight against each other. The ones who survived the slaughter ran as fast and as far away from the battlefield as they could. A battle cry was the beginning of the successful war campaign.

The shout—or battle cry—is not a new strategy, but the Holy Spirit is emphasizing the sound and intensity of this shout through many seasoned voices in this time. In warfare, there is a time to stay silent—but there is also a time to shout. The Holy Spirit–inspired shout releases the sound of now that, time and time again, precedes a great breakthrough to victory.

Shouting Down the Enemy

The enemy is noisy. He makes noisy threats and breathes noisy lies. Sometimes, you just have to shout him down, as old-time Pentecostal preachers would say. The sound of now through a shout breaks down demonic walls blocking the way to your promised land.

We see this concept in Joshua 6:1–5, 20–21:

> Now Jericho was securely shut up because of the children of Israel; none went out, and none came in. And the LORD said to Joshua: "See! I have given Jericho into your hand, its king, and the mighty men of valor. You shall march around the city, all you men of war; you shall go all around the city once. This you shall do six days. And seven priests shall bear seven trumpets of rams' horns before the ark. But the seventh day you shall march around the city seven times, and the priests shall blow the trumpets. It shall come to pass, when they make a long blast with the ram's horn, and when you hear the sound of the trumpet, that all the people shall shout with a great shout; then the wall of the city will fall down flat. And the people shall go up every man straight before him."
>
> . . . So the people shouted when the priests blew the trumpets. And it happened when the people heard the sound of the trumpet, and the people shouted with a great shout, that

the wall fell down flat. Then the people went up into the city, every man straight before him, and they took the city. And they utterly destroyed all that was in the city, both man and woman, young and old, ox and sheep and donkey, with the edge of the sword.

Joshua got the breakthrough with a shout. The Israelites literally shouted the walls down. It may be time to shout down the walls holding back your healing or your financial breakthrough. You may have to shout at the mountain representing the obstacles to walking in the prophetic life God wants you to live.

This is a more intense approach than speaking to your mountain, which is a familiar biblical image. Jesus said, "For assuredly, I say to you, whoever says to this mountain, 'Be removed and be cast into the sea,' and does not doubt in his heart, but believes that those things he says will be done, he will have whatever he says" (Mark 11:23).

Maybe you are facing an intimidating mountain. Maybe you are staring at an entire mountain range—problem after problem after problem mounting up against you. Whether there is a single mountain or more mountains than you can count, speaking is always the right strategy—but sometimes you have to raise your voice a little louder and actually shout at it!

Let's look at Zechariah. An angel prophesied a word from the Lord for the prophet to give to Zerubbabel, the governor of Judah who had laid the foundation for the Temple. Imagine the resistance Zerubbabel faced in this effort!

"This is the word of the LORD to Zerubbabel: 'Not by might nor by power, but by My Spirit,' says the LORD of hosts. 'Who are you, O great mountain? Before Zerubbabel you shall become a plain! And he shall bring forth the capstone with shouts of "Grace, grace to it!""

Zechariah 4:6–7

So there are times to speak to the mountain, but there are also times to shout at the mountain. The Holy Spirit will always give you the right strategy so you can make the right sound.

Holding On to Your Promises

Sometimes when your promised land is in sight, the enemy seems to grow too fierce, and it appears that you are out of options for the miracle breakthrough you need in order to hold fast. It is at these times that a shout comes forth that moves the Lord to take up your battle Himself.

Abijah, ruler over the kingdom of Judah, and the warriors who stood with him can attest to this. War broke out between Abijah and King Jeroboam, who sat on the throne of the rebellious and rival northern tribes of the kingdom of Israel. Jeroboam had twice as many foot soldiers as Abijah, and threatened to take over Judah, land that God had promised to David forever (see 2 Chronicles 13:5).

But Abijah had a secret weapon: Not only was he protecting his godly inheritance, but Judah had remained faithful to Jehovah. Jeroboam was a wicked king, and it seemed he had the upper hand and was winning the war—until Judah let out a shout.

Read the account in 2 Chronicles 13:13–18:

Jeroboam caused an ambush to go around behind them; so they were in front of Judah, and the ambush was behind them. And when Judah looked around, to their surprise the battle line was at both front and rear; and they cried out to the Lord, and the priests sounded the trumpets. Then the men of Judah gave a shout; and as the men of Judah shouted, it happened that God struck Jeroboam and all Israel before Abijah and Judah. And the children of Israel fled before Judah, and God delivered them into their hand. Then Abijah and his people struck them with a great slaughter; so five hundred thousand choice men of Israel fell slain. Thus the children of Israel were subdued at that time; and the children of Judah prevailed, because they relied on the Lord God of their fathers.

It was a desperate cry—the shout of faith—that secured the promised land for Abijah and Judah that day. I can imagine the shout of faith turned into a shout of joy.

When the dust settles on the battle and you have emerged with the breakthrough for your promised land, remember to do this one thing: Shout for joy! Or as the psalmist put it, "Shout to God with the voice of triumph!" (Psalm 47:1).

10

The Sound of Now in Music Brings Healing and Deliverance

When I was a teenager, I was more than a little melancholy. I listened to morose music, proclaiming the depressive lyrics over my life against the backdrops of synthesizers and bass guitars. Unknowingly, I filled my mind with TV shows, movies and magazine images inspired by the prince of the power of the air.

Many teenagers—and even some Christian youth—do the same today. The enemy has erected a stronghold in arts, entertainment and culture because he knows the power of sight and sound. He knows that our eyes, ears and mouths are gates through which he can influence our souls. He knows that the power of death and life are in the tongue and uses music and media to shape our thoughts, words (sounds) and, ultimately, actions.

Although Satan, who once led worship in heaven, has strategically infiltrated the sounds of this generation and polluted the media, I am encouraged to see God raising up believers to use sound to turn the hearts of lost souls to the Father. I am inspired by the creativity of projects that can cross cultural and generational barriers to make the sound of the Gospel—the ultimate sound of healing and deliverance—plain.

God is inspiring believers in this hour with divine ideas, witty inventions and skillful hands to bring sounds of life through music and media. We are also hearing more about how sound brings healing and deliverance. Indeed, artists are taking a second look at music as a means to heal the soul and body.

Decades ago, church congregations sang hymns until the truth of Scripture about God as our healer or our strong tower went down deep into their hearts; their minds were renewed and bondages were broken. Over the years I have seen massive breakthroughs—captives set free without any-one laying a hand on them—when the Holy Spirit moved in worship to the extent that it replaced the morning sermon.

I have seen firsthand how the playing of a violin causes people to release deep emotional pain at the altar, and I have read the testimonies of many others who have seen deaf ears open, cancer healed and migraines go as music ushered them into a place in the glory of God where miracles happen.

Nature reveals the artistry of God, but so do our own bodies. I like the wording of Ephesians 2:10 in the New Living Translation: "For we are God's masterpiece. He has created us anew in Christ Jesus, so we can do the good things he planned for us long ago." Not only does God speak to us through sounds expressed in music, art and media, but He also considers us a work of art. After all, we were created in His image, and He continues to form us into the image of Christ.

Stories in the Bible confirm that sound unlocks healing and deliverance. The Canaanite woman's faith, spoken aloud persistently in the face of seeming rejection, moved Jesus to deliver her demon-possessed daughter even though she was not part of the Abrahamic covenant—and the girl was set free immediately (see Matthew 15:28). Hezekiah's desperate sound in prayer helped him escape an early death due to a boil on his body—and God gave him another fifteen years to live (see 2 Kings 20:3–6).

Words are not always needed. Sometimes the sound of now is transmitted through music itself. In other words, there is healing and delivering power in sound. Not just any sound—the right sound at the right time. Secular medical science is proving what we already know from reading the pages of the Bible. Sound waves in the right kind of music can break through where medicine cannot.

Healing Power in Sound

Earlier in this book, we focused on the art and science of sound. We have come full circle because it is not just words that have power, but other sounds as well. An entire field of medicine centers on music therapy. Music therapists are skilled musicians who understand the intricacies of how music can have impact on emotions to relax, motivate and even help people heal.

"It's fascinating and powerful to think that music, something that has been floating around in our environment forever—that this natural, omnipresent human activity—has demonstrable benefit as treatment,"[1] says Sarah Hoover, D.M.A., co-director of the Johns Hopkins Center for Music and Medicine. Indeed, music has been floating around since our omnipresent God created it, and clearly, it is not just for our entertainment.

According to research done by Harvard Medical School, music therapy has myriad benefits:

> Those who listened to music in the operating room reported less discomfort during their procedure. Hearing music in the recovery room lowered the use of opioid painkillers. . . . Listening to music [can] quell nausea and vomiting for patients receiving chemotherapy. [2]

The Harvard research also indicates that music therapy improves quality of life for dementia patients and can help restore lost speech in patients recovering from a stroke or traumatic brain injury. Lisa Hartling, Ph.D., professor of pediatrics at the University of Alberta and lead author of a pediatric study about the impact of music on patients, reveals this: "There is growing scientific evidence showing that the brain responds to music in very specific ways."[3]

How, exactly, does this work? Ashford University in San Diego reports what happens to the brain when we listen to music:

> One of the first things that happens when music enters our brains is the triggering of pleasure centers that release dopamine, a neurotransmitter that makes you feel happy. This response is so quick, the brain can even anticipate the most pleasurable peaks in familiar music and prime itself with an early dopamine rush.[4]

The article also reports that music can boost pro-immunity antibodies, help energize mood, help treat depression and diseases, and reduce stress.

Songs of Deliverance

You have probably heard these poetic words by William Congreve (1697): "Music hath charms to soothe the savage breast" (often rendered as *beast*). Both the original (trusting *Bartlett's Familiar Quotations*) and the misquote remind me of the picture in the Bible of the ruddy young shepherd David. The multitalented youth was not only accurate with a sling and a stone, but he also played stringed musical instruments.

Consider this telling account:

> The Spirit of the LORD departed from Saul, and a distressing spirit from the LORD troubled him. And Saul's servants said to him, "Surely, a distressing spirit from God is troubling you. Let our master now command your servants, who are before you, to seek out a man who is a skillful player on the harp. And it shall be that he will play it with his hand when the distressing spirit from God is upon you, and you shall be well."
>
> 1 Samuel 16:14–16

Notice something here: Saul's attendants not only had revelation that a demon was harassing Saul, but they also understood the sound of now through music to cause that devil to flee. The Old Testament has no instances of people casting out demons in the same way that Jesus and His followers did in the New Testament, but we do see evidence of a deliverance ministry through the right sound. Notice how Saul's attendant did not recommend just any harpist. He was looking for a skillful player. It had to be the right sound. Let's continue with the account:

> So Saul said to his servants, "Provide me now a man who can play well, and bring him to me." Then one of the servants

answered and said, "Look, I have seen a son of Jesse the Bethlehemite, who is skillful in playing, a mighty man of valor, a man of war, prudent in speech, and a handsome person; and the LORD is with him."

. . . So David came to Saul and stood before him. And he loved him greatly, and he became his armorbearer. Then Saul sent to Jesse, saying, "Please let David stand before me, for he has found favor in my sight." And so it was, whenever the spirit from God was upon Saul, that David would take a harp and play it with his hand. Then Saul would become refreshed and well, and the distressing spirit would depart from him.

1 Samuel 16:17–18, 21–23

We see a confirmation of the delivering power of song in Psalm 32:7: "You are my hiding place; You shall preserve me from trouble; You shall surround me with songs of deliverance." That is the bedrock of worship theology on how sound can set the captives free. I might not have believed it, entirely, if I had not seen it with my own eyes in revival meetings.

Can Music Set the Stage for Miracles?

Science proves the benefits of music on the soul and body. But can music actually set the stage for miracles? Do specific sounds and frequencies invite God's healing power into our atmospheres? Is it as much about faith to believe that music carries the healing power of God as it is the music itself?

I attended a conference a few years ago when I first heard a violin player ministering to the Lord with her instrument. The anointing was undeniable. It was almost as if the entire congregation was caught up in an ecstatic experience. Without anyone moving, people burst into tears and cried out in praise to God. Indeed, the sound of the music elicited a sound from the people—and it seemed that the combination of those sounds bred miracles.

Since God created music, and everything He created is good and comes from love, it is not hard to believe that music has healing and delivering power. And there is plenty of biblical evidence to support this claim. The sound of David's harp delivering Saul from tormenting spirits may be the most obvious example.

But it is not the only one. The apostles Paul and Silas were imprisoned, beaten and bloodied, but they started praying and singing hymns to God. The sound of their combined prayers and praise caused God to move heaven and earth to set them free. In fact, God even delivered the keeper of the prison and his entire household (see Acts 16:25–34)!

Healing music is more than a trend. It is more than a scientific theory. The power in music to heal and deliver is a Kingdom reality seen in the pages of Scripture. Music is part of the sound-of-now equation that moves our hearts to cry out in what becomes a symphony of faith in the ears of God. Music helps us lift up our praise and worship, soothes our fears of disease and death, and comforts our hearts. Music and the sound of now go hand in hand to produce miraculous breakthroughs in spirit, soul and body.

11

The Sound of Now Births the New Thing

Travail is no stranger to me, and I am no stranger to travail. Although there are many aspects of travail—and many outcomes—God has travailed through me to birth things in my life that my eye had not seen, nor my ear heard—nor that had even entered into my heart. With the sound of now that comes through travailing prayer, God birthed new things I never would have thought to ask for—and might not have asked for because it did not seem possible to me.

When I was editor of *Charisma* magazine, I worked to introduce new voices and new faces to the publication—both in print and online. I labored with Christ to bring a new prophetic mantle to the venerated charismatic periodical. I had the opportunity to converse with many great leaders in the prophetic movement and beyond during those years. One afternoon in 2016, working from my office at home, I had conversations with two leaders in the apostolic-prophetic movement about the state of the prophetic movement. The

101

conclusion: There were some definite challenges we needed to address.

At one point after the calls as I was heading to my office, the Holy Spirit led me to pray. Honestly, this was not the best time to pray. We were on a printer deadline for the magazine, and missing a deadline would come at a heavy financial cost to the company. When I informed the Holy Spirit of this reality, it seemed not to move Him. He continued to urge me to pray. I got down on my knees right there and knelt over a couch to pray. In my mind, I planned to pray for a few minutes, then go back to the office to get the magazine out, and later resume praying.

Well, I did pray and I did go back to the office, but before I sat in front of my computer I went into sudden intense travail. That travail lasted about two hours and left a puddle of tears on my hardwood floor. I literally felt the Holy Spirit's agony over issues in some of the camps in the prophetic movement. He showed me things to come—He told me what to expect if there was no prophetic reset within five years. He spoke of false prophets rising and Jezebel's influence. When the travail finally ended, I was wiped out (but He did give me grace to finish sending off the magazine afterward).

What did that birth? Many things, starting with my first School of the Prophets that was organized and established in just six weeks and launched with a full house. It also birthed the Ignite prophetic network, a company of prophets and prophetic believers contending for a pure prophetic flow, learning, growing, praying—and doing prophetic life together. The birthing was in stages as later God sent me into other nations to establish prophetic training and finally led me to set up the Global Prophetic Center where the nations can come to me since I cannot go to every nation. I believe this is just the beginning.

The Sound That Births

The sound of now births a new thing. The sound of now sometimes manifests as travail. If you have never heard the term, let me assure you it is biblical. In fact, there are at least thirty Scriptures dealing with travail. Travail as it relates to the sound of now is a Spirit-inspired act that brings Holy Spirit power to bear to bring forth something that does not yet exist.

Put another way, just as travail in Scripture is sometimes used to speak of natural birth, it is also used to speak of spiritual birth. Paul wrote, "My little children, of whom I travail in birth again until Christ be formed in you" (Galatians 4:19 KJV). Obviously Paul was not speaking of a natural birth but a spiritual birthing.

The Greek word for *travail* in this verse means "to bring forth, bear, suffer birth-pangs" and generally speaks of a woman giving literal birth. In the King James Version of the Bible it is translates as "bring forth" most of the time. The Hebrew word for *travail* also implies "to birth or bring forth." The dictionary definition of *bring forth* is "to cause to exist or occur."

James Goll defines travail like this:

Travail is a form of intense intercession given by the Holy Spirit whereby an individual or group is gripped by a gestating promise that grips God's heart. The individual or group labors with Him in prayer so that the new life can come forth. . . .

Travail takes place after you have carried something in your heart for a period of time. It comes on you suddenly. It is preceded by nurturing the promise; later the strategic time comes to push that promise forth through the prayer canal. Finally you realize that the promise has been born, and you are greatly relieved when the delivery is over![1]

Paul discusses this spiritual practice in Romans 8:26–29 (MEV):

> Likewise, the Spirit helps us in our weaknesses, for we do not know what to pray for as we ought, but the Spirit Himself intercedes for us with groanings too deep for words. He who searches the hearts knows what the mind of the Spirit is, because He intercedes for the saints according to the will of God.

These "groanings too deep for words" are one manifestation of travailing prayer.

Travail Resurrects Dead Things

In his book *Intercessory Prayer*, Dutch Sheets breaks down *travail* in a simple way:

The Holy Spirit is involved.

It is associated with spiritual reproduction.

It aids in the maturing process of believers.

It can be very intense, involving fervency, tears and even groaning.

Assuming Christ was in travail at Lazarus's tomb and Elijah was in birthing prayer on the mountain, it is involved in producing miracles, not just the new birth.[2]

In other words, travail releases a sound of now that can bring breakthrough. The Holy Spirit does the birthing, but He does it through us. He did it through Jesus and Elijah. He can do it through you. You cannot make it happen. You cannot decide to travail. What you can do is yield to the Holy Spirit when travail comes upon you. You can sometimes discern the onset of travail as grief over something that is out of line with God's will. When travail came upon me over the prophetic movement, I felt deep grief first. This is what happened with Jesus over Lazarus.

Jesus knew Lazarus was sick, but He did not go to His friend's rescue. Scripture tells us He waited purposely until Lazarus died so that people would believe He was the Resurrection and the Life. Lazarus's sisters, Mary and Martha, were upset that Jesus did not come sooner. When He arrived, they each met Him. When Jesus saw Mary—and the Jews who came with her—weeping, He groaned in His spirit and was troubled (see John 11:33). Remember, Romans 8 speaks of groanings too deep for words in relation to the Holy Spirit interceding through us. When Jesus saw where they had laid Lazarus, He wept. Let's look at the miracle breakthrough that followed:

> Then Jesus, again groaning in Himself, came to the tomb. It was a cave, and a stone lay against it. Jesus said, "Take away the stone."
>
> Martha, the sister of him who was dead, said to Him, "Lord, by this time there is a stench, for he has been dead four days."
>
> Jesus said to her, "Did I not say to you that if you would believe you would see the glory of God?" Then they took away the stone from the place where the dead man was lying. And Jesus lifted up His eyes and said, "Father, I thank You that You have heard Me. And I know that You always hear

Me, but because of the people who are standing by I said this, that they may believe that You sent Me." Now when He had said these things, He cried with a loud voice, "Lazarus, come forth!" And he who had died came out bound hand and foot with graveclothes, and his face was wrapped with a cloth. Jesus said to them, "Loose him, and let him go."

John 11:38–44

Notice how Jesus groaned, then He sighed and wept, then He groaned again, then He cried with a loud voice. I believe Jesus was in travail. Remember, not all travail is as dramatic as what I experienced in my office. Some travail is more of an inward experience. Natural emotions do not lead you into travail, but spiritual emotions do. When God's emotions touch your emotions, sometimes you enter into travail to bring life to dead things.

"Many times travail can be so strong that it seems to overwhelm the intercessor," said Cindy Jacobs, co-founder of Generals International. She continued,

> Those around need to intercede for the one in travail if this happens in a group situation. We need to help bear the burden in prayer. . . . We also need to watch after that one by binding the enemy from entering into the travail.
>
> One word of caution. The Holy Spirit will rule over our emotions in a time of travail. We must be sure that we do not let our emotions run wild. Intercessors need to walk in the fruit of self-control.[3]

Travail Brings Breakthrough

The prophet Elijah announced a drought, and Israel experienced famine. After the showdown at Mount Carmel, Elijah made another prophetic announcement to Ahab: "Go up, eat and drink; for there is the sound of abundance of rain" (1 Kings 18:41). Elijah heard a sound in His spirit that caused him to enter into travail. He must have been pretty convincing because Ahab went up to eat and drink while Elijah went up to the top of Carmel.

Look what happened next: "Then he bowed down on the ground, and put his face between his knees, and said to his servant, 'Go up now, look toward the sea'" (1 Kings 18:42–43).

Elijah was in the same position in which Hebrew women birthed babies. He was in a birthing position because the Holy Spirit had revealed a sound in the spirit—the sound of abundance of rain—that demanded a sound in the natural before the rain could fall from the sky.

We do not know how long Elijah travailed before he told his servant to go take a look. The servant replied, "'There is nothing.' And seven times [Elijah] said, 'Go again.' Then it came to pass the seventh time, that he said, 'There is a cloud, as small as a man's hand, rising out of the sea!'" (1 Kings 18:43–44).

Elijah was persistent, which was the key to the breakthrough. We will look more at persistence in a later chapter. If Elijah had given up after sending his servant back just five or six times, the nation of Israel would not have seen its breakthrough, and Elijah's prophetic announcement would have fallen to the ground.

> So he said, "Go up, say to Ahab, 'Prepare your chariot, and go down before the rain stops you.'"
> Now it happened in the meantime that the sky became black with clouds and wind, and there was a heavy rain. So Ahab rode away and went to Jezreel. Then the hand of the

LORD came upon Elijah; and he girded up his loins and ran ahead of Ahab to the entrance of Jezreel.

1 Kings 18:44–46

This was no little drizzle. This travail brought forth heavy rain—and abundance of rain indeed. *The KJV Old Testament Hebrew Lexicon* gives us insight into this rain. *Heavy* in this verse means "large in magnitude and extent, great and loud in sound." Elijah heard loud rain in the spirit and birthed forth loud rain in the natural through Spirit-led travail. Rain broke the curse of famine and served as a blessing to a thirsty land.

Again, you cannot decide to travail, but you can decide to cooperate with the Holy Spirit. We read in 1 Thessalonians 5:19 that Paul the apostle urges us not to quench the Holy Spirit—not to stifle, extinguish, restrain or turn away from His movements. Travail can be a painful, sweaty experience, but the results will be well worth it. You may not immediately know what breakthrough you birthed because in God's timeline He can work through you now for a future breakthrough.

12

The Sound of Now Releases Breakthrough Angels

An angel named Breakthrough whisked by.

I was ministering with Cindy Jacobs at a private event called Breakthrough. She asked me to help her prophesy over the attendees. I brought two of my staff to pray for me as I prayed for others. As I started releasing the word of the Lord, suddenly I saw an angel whisk by. It was so fast and sudden—angels can move faster than the speed of light—that I did a double take.

I turned to the two women, one on my left and one on my right, and asked, "Did you see that?" They both affirmed that they had seen an angel move through. The Lord told me the angel's name was Breakthrough. The next day at Awakening House of Prayer's afternoon service, we had a massive breakthrough. Toward the end of the service, the Lord told me the breakthrough angel had followed me to church. I had never experienced anything like it before.

If that were not enough, the breakthrough angel followed me home (though I did not immediately know it). On my *Mornings with the Holy Spirit* prayer broadcast the next morning, we had a massive breakthrough. Toward the end of the broadcast, the Holy Spirit told me the breakthrough angel was still with me. He has never left.

The Lord led me to prophesy these words on that broadcast to listeners who were holding on to promises. I heard the Lord say,

> *I am dispatching angels of breakthrough on assignment on your behalf because your prayer answers have been resisted. Yes, you've been resisted in lifting them up, but you've broken through that resistance. You've been resisted in crying out to Me. The enemy has bombarded your mind with imaginations and with thoughts and feelings that your pleas are not making any difference—that they are not doing any good. I have heard your cries, and just as the prince of Persia resisted the angel that I sent to deliver prayer answers to Daniel, I have seen the resistance in the heavenlies to receiving your prayer answers.*
>
> *But I have sent an angel of breakthrough to assist. I have an angel of breakthrough on assignment. I have sent angels of breakthrough, indeed, to make sure that the words you've released—even the prophetic words you've warred with—come to pass. I have been watching over those words to perform them. I have been watching over those prophecies spoken over your life to perform them.*
>
> *And the angels are coming to execute My word. They have hearkened to the voice of My word coming out of your mouth. Every time you confessed Scripture, every time you confessed those prophecies—those things I spoke to your heart—you activated angels. Now angels of breakthrough are coming for many in this season where breakthrough has eluded you, breakthrough has escaped you, breakthrough*

seems to be running away from you, but I say blessings will chase you down and overtake you because I am sending angelic assistance your way.

The breakthrough angels came as these prophetic words went forth. Understand this: When the Bible says that the power of death and life is in the tongue (see Proverbs 18:21), that is what it means. When you release words in the spirit, both angels and demons are standing by to execute those words in your life—either for you or against you.

Angels All around Us

Angels are just as real as you and I. The word *angel* is mentioned in the Bible more than 280 times. That is an average of about four times for each of the 66 books of the Bible. If the Lord were to pull back the curtain blocking our sight of the spiritual realm, you would see angels all around you. What you cannot see is just as real as what you can see.

Angels are all around us, but what exactly are angels? Angels are spirit beings. Speaking of angels, Hebrews 1:14 tells us, "Are they not all ministering spirits sent forth to minister for those who will inherit salvation?" Angels have all sorts of assignments, but they are essentially messengers. The root word for *angel* in both Hebrew and Greek is *messenger*.

Every angel is not a breakthrough angel, but the Bible tells of angels with many functions who helped bring breakthrough to the heirs of salvation. John 5:4 tells of a healing angel who stirred up the waters in a pool near one of Jerusalem's gates; whoever first got into the water was healed from whatever disease he had. It was not the angel doing the healing, but the angel set the stage for healing.

We see guardian angels, also called angels of protection, manifest in the pages of the Bible. The concept of guardian angels comes from Jesus' words as recorded in Matthew 18:10: "Take heed that you do not despise one of these little ones, for I say to you that in heaven their angels always see the face of My Father who is in heaven."

Forerunner angels go before us to clear a path, as seen in Exodus 23:23 when the Lord told Moses, "My Angel will go before you and bring you in to the Amorites and the Hittites and the Perizzites and the Canaanites and the Hivites and the Jebusites; and I will cut them off."

Angels Respond to Your Words

Angels do come at the sound of your words. You can release breakthrough with your mouth and watch breakthrough angels go to work. We do not command angels; Jesus is the Captain of the Hosts. But when we speak the Word of God, whether that is the logos Word, a true prophetic word, or something in line with Scripture (Jesus is not religious and legalistic), I believe angels' ears perk up.

I believe this because I have meditated on Psalm 103:20–21 for many years: "Bless the LORD, you His angels, who excel in strength, who do His word, heeding the voice of His word. Bless the LORD, all you His hosts, you ministers of His, who do His pleasure." Angels are strong and able to execute God's Word, which is God's will. Meditating on various translations will give you faith to believe for breakthrough angels to work with your words.

The New Living Translation tells us, "Praise the LORD, you angels, you mighty ones who carry out his plans, listening for each of his commands. Yes, praise the LORD, you armies of angels who serve him and do his will!" The Passion Translation puts it this way: "Bless the Lord, all his messengers of power, for you are his mighty heroes who listen intently to the voice of his word to do it. Bless and praise the Lord, you mighty warriors, ministers who serve him well and fulfill his desires." And *The Message* says this: "So bless God, you angels, ready and able to fly at his bidding, quick to hear and do what he says. Bless God, all you armies of angels, alert to respond to whatever he wills."

If you want more breakthrough in your life, learn to work with the angels. Again, *you do not command them*. You are not the boss of the angels. But you can give them something to work with. You can pore through Scripture to find and release the right sound that attracts the angels to pick up the word and run with it—and war with it. Angels do God's bidding, but when God gives you a word to fight with, the warring angels themselves will go for you physically into places in the second heaven and battle the resistance to your breakthrough.

Warring Angels Bring Breakthrough

Warring angels also bring your breakthrough. Daniel's story may be familiar to you, but it is worth recounting. Daniel was in captivity in Babylon and refused to compromise his beliefs. He was a student of Scripture, discerning that the times he was living in were the days Jeremiah wrote about in his prophetic chronicles.

In the first year of Darius the Mede, understanding the time and season, Daniel went into prayer:

> Then I set my face toward the Lord God to make request by prayer and supplications, with fasting, sackcloth, and ashes.

And I prayed to the LORD my God, and made confession, and said, "O Lord, great and awesome God, who keeps His covenant and mercy with those who love Him, and with those who keep His commandments, we have sinned and committed iniquity, we have done wickedly and rebelled, even by departing from Your precepts and Your judgments. Neither have we heeded Your servants the prophets, who spoke in Your name to our kings and our princes, to our fathers and all the people of the land. O Lord, righteousness belongs to You, but to us shame of face, as it is this day—to the men of Judah, to the inhabitants of Jerusalem and all Israel, those near and those far off in all the countries to which You have driven them, because of the unfaithfulness which they have committed against You."

Daniel 9:3–7

Daniel continued in repentance, acknowledging Jeremiah's prophecies and crying out with the sound of now for divine mercy:

"O Lord, according to all Your righteousness, I pray, let Your anger and Your fury be turned away from Your city Jerusalem, Your holy mountain; because for our sins, and for the iniquities of our fathers, Jerusalem and Your people are a reproach to all those around us. Now therefore, our God, hear the prayer of Your servant, and his supplications, and for the Lord's sake cause Your face to shine on Your sanctuary, which is desolate. O my God, incline Your ear and hear; open Your eyes and see our desolations, and the city which is called by Your name; for we do not present our supplications before You because of our righteous deeds, but because of Your great mercies. O Lord, hear! O Lord, forgive! O Lord, listen and act! Do not delay for Your own sake, my God, for Your city and Your people are called by Your name."

Daniel 9:16–19

What happened after Daniel released the sound of now through repentance is astounding. While he was on his face interceding for Jerusalem, the angel Gabriel showed up in the evening hours. Gabriel gave him a message, known to us as "the seventy-weeks prophecy," which will culminate in the end times and the coming of the Messiah.

Later, in a vision he was given while standing on the bank of the Tigris, Daniel saw a "man" who gave him further understanding regarding the revelations he had received. After fasting for three weeks, Daniel encountered the angel who had been working to bring answers to his prayers since the first day, for, said the angel, his prayers had been heard:

> Suddenly, a hand touched me, which made me tremble on my knees and on the palms of my hands. And he said to me, "O Daniel, man greatly beloved, understand the words that I speak to you, and stand upright, for I have now been sent to you." While he was speaking this word to me, I stood trembling.
>
> Then he said to me, "Do not fear, Daniel, for from the first day that you set your heart to understand, and to humble yourself before your God, your words were heard; and I have come because of your words. But the prince of the kingdom of Persia withstood me twenty-one days; and behold, Michael, one of the chief princes, came to help me, for I had been left alone there with the kings of Persia. Now I have come to make you understand what will happen to your people in the latter days, for the vision refers to many days yet to come."
>
> Daniel 10:10–14

The battle was not over. The angel told Daniel that he had to return to fight with the prince of Persia—the principality that was ruling over Persia—but this was a breakthrough revelation. Daniel knew his words had been heard and that God's mighty angels would ultimately prevail.

You may not have an angelic encounter to inform you that your prayer answer is in process, but you do not need one. We can have confidence in prayer according to 1 John 5:14–15: "Now this is the confidence that we have in Him, that if we ask anything according to His will, He hears us. And if we know that He hears us, whatever we ask, we know that we have the petitions that we have asked of Him."

13

When the Sound of Now Is Tears

Have you ever cried yourself to sleep? Sometimes, you cannot find the words to pray, and the pain gets in the way of a proper petition. When you cannot praise your way through, your tears can release the sound of now that moves God's heart with compassion. These are not just any tears—tears of self-pity will not move God. But God hears your tears when they come from a place of desperation that believes He can move, even when you are overcome with sorrow.

Yes, God hears your tears, and your tears become your prayers. Your tears become your intercession. Corey Russell, a former International House of Prayer of Kansas City staffer, once preached a message on tears in which he described this emotional state as one that occurs when you come face-to-face with your human inability to change anything yourself. It is God who brings you to that place.

King David was a warrior, but he was also man of tears. David was so distraught at times he watered his bed with tears.

David cried out for deliverance. David cried out for mercy. David cried when his cruel spiritual father, Saul, died. He cried when his best friend, Jonathan, died. He cried when his son Absalom died. David wept at the grave of Abner. He wrote, "I am weary with my groaning; all night I make my bed swim; I drench my couch with my tears" (Psalm 6:6).

Try Tears

God actually puts our tears in a bottle (see Psalm 56:8). The story is well known of the Salvation Army field worker who inquired of founder William Booth, "Sir, we tried every method; what shall we do?"

William Booth replied, "Try tears."

You cannot actually try tears in the sense that you make yourself cry to manipulate God. But you can yield to tears when they come. Over and over again, David let his tears do the talking. At one point, he admitted his tears were his food day and night as his enemies mocked his faith in God (see Psalm 42:3).

"Hear my prayer, O Lord, and give ear to my cry; do not be silent at my tears; for I am a stranger with You, a sojourner, as all my fathers were" (Psalm 39:12). Can you hear the desperation in that verse?

"Tears appeal to the Divine pity in an especial way," offers *The Pulpit Commentary*. "Hence, being so weak and dependent, we may the more confidently claim God's pity."[1] The tears that release the sound of now are tears that flow when we come to the end of ourselves—and God is moved with compassion.

In every account in Scripture that Jesus was moved with compassion, a miracle occurred. Consider the widow at Nain:

Now it happened, the day after, that He went into a city called Nain; and many of His disciples went with Him, and a large crowd. And when He came near the gate of the city, behold, a dead man was being carried out, the only son of his mother; and she was a widow. And a large crowd from the city was with her. When the Lord saw her, He had compassion on her and said to her, "Do not weep." Then He came and touched the open coffin, and those who carried him stood still. And He said, "Young man, I say to you, arise." So he who was dead sat up and began to speak. And He presented him to his mother.

Luke 7:11–15

Jesus also raised Lazarus from the dead in the midst of Mary's and Martha's weeping. Tears do not bring back everyone who dies, but for whatever reason the widow's tears caused Jesus to move in pity. And our tears can cause God to move with compassion to resurrect things that look dead in our lives.

The psalms also record breakthroughs that came in the wake of tears. One psalmist wrote, "You have delivered my soul from death, my eyes from tears, and my feet from falling" (Psalm 116:8). In other words, he stopped weeping when he started winning. Another psalmist assures us, "Those who sow in tears shall reap in joy" (Psalm 126:5). How can that be unless our tears are our prayers? It was David himself who promised, "Weeping may endure for a night, but joy comes in the morning" (Psalm 30:5). Joy comes because the prayer is answered. Remember, these words of Jesus: "Ask, and you will receive, that your joy may be made full" (John 16:24).

The Sound of Now Breaks Barrenness

Hannah was barren. Although her husband, Elkanah, gave her a double portion at the annual offering of sacrifices, material possessions did not satisfy her ache for a child. Elkanah's other wife, Peninnah, who had many sons and daughters, made fun of Hannah because she could not have children.

Year after year, Hannah wept and fasted when it was time to make the annual offering, and her husband simply could not understand it. So Hannah was provoked, misunderstood, bitter, in anguish and barren:

> Elkanah her husband said to her, "Hannah, why do you weep? Why do you not eat? And why is your heart grieved? Am I not better to you than ten sons?"
>
> So Hannah arose after they had finished eating and drinking in Shiloh. Now Eli the priest was sitting on the seat by the doorpost of the tabernacle of the LORD. And she was in bitterness of soul, and prayed to the LORD and wept in anguish.
>
> 1 Samuel 1:8–10

Have you ever felt that way? In her desperation and through her tears, Hannah made a vow to the Lord. If the Lord would give her a male child, she promised she would dedicate him to the Lord's service all the days of his life, and he would take a Nazarite vow, meaning he would be wholly consecrated to the Lord. In other words, if God would give her a baby boy she would give him back to the Lord. She just wanted to see the curse broken.

Unfortunately, Hannah continued to be misunderstood. As she was praying, the priest Eli watched her mouth moving but heard no words coming out and thought she was drunk. He rebuked Hannah in her moment of desperation. Hannah explained to Eli, in essence, that she was releasing the sound of now:

> Hannah answered and said, "No, my lord, I am a woman of sorrowful spirit. I have drunk neither wine nor intoxicating drink, but have poured out my soul before the LORD. Do not consider your maidservant a wicked woman, for out of the abundance of my complaint and grief I have spoken until now."
>
> Then Eli answered and said, "Go in peace, and the God of Israel grant your petition which you have asked of Him."
>
> And she said, "Let your maidservant find favor in your sight." So the woman went her way and ate, and her face was no longer sad.
>
> 1 Samuel 1:15–18

I believe Hannah felt the breakthrough in her spirit. How do I know? Until now, her habit was to weep and not to eat throughout this season. Now, her face was no longer sad and she ate. The tears stopped when they accomplished their purpose in the spirit. You cannot manufacture this kind of tears. God brings you to this place. But it is a real phenomenon that shifts things in the spirit.

We see the outcome: Hannah birthed Samuel and fulfilled her vow to the Lord. Samuel helped restore the prophetic voice in his generation and raised up prophets to continue after him. What is more, Hannah had five more children over the years. That is more than the double her husband gave her each year at offering time. Her tears released a sound of now that broke barrenness.

Job's Tears

There is a plant called Job's Tears. You have to cry a lot to have a plant named after your tears! "My friends scorn me; my eyes pour out tears to God" (Job 16:20). Job had plenty of reasons to cry. He sustained one of the worst demonic attacks we see in the pages of the Bible, despite the reality that Scripture calls him a man who "was blameless and upright, and one who feared God and shunned evil" (Job 1:1).

Look with fresh eyes at the sudden attack Job endured:

> Now there was a day when his sons and daughters were eating and drinking wine in their oldest brother's house; and a messenger came to Job and said, "The oxen were plowing and the donkeys feeding beside them, when the Sabeans raided them and took them away—indeed they have killed the servants with the edge of the sword; and I alone have escaped to tell you!"
>
> While he was still speaking, another also came and said, "The fire of God fell from heaven and burned up the sheep and the servants, and consumed them; and I alone have escaped to tell you!"
>
> While he was still speaking, another also came and said, "The Chaldeans formed three bands, raided the camels and took them away, yes, and killed the servants with the edge of the sword; and I alone have escaped to tell you!"
>
> While he was still speaking, another also came and said, "Your sons and daughters were eating and drinking wine in their oldest brother's house, and suddenly a great wind came from across the wilderness and struck the four corners of the house, and it fell on the young people, and they are dead; and I alone have escaped to tell you!"
>
> Job 1:13–19

You have heard it said bad things happen in threes. This is the incident that sparked that saying—Job lost his livestock, his servants and his children. Job later lost his health and had sores all over his body. It is no wonder his face was flushed from weeping, and the shadow of death was on his eyelids (see Job 16:16). It is not surprising his harp "turned to mourning, and [his] flute to the voice of those who weep" (Job 30:31).

Job defended himself against his friends, who offered many reasons why calamity had come to his house, but his self-defense did not move God. In fact, God challenged Job's mind-set. It was not until Job repented before God for his attitude that breakthrough dawned. Whether or not he repented in tears, God had collected Job's tears in a bottle and was moved with compassion to restore Job after his suffering.

Job 42:12–17 tells the victorious end of his story:

> Now the LORD blessed the latter days of Job more than his beginning; for he had fourteen thousand sheep, six thousand camels, one thousand yoke of oxen, and one thousand female donkeys. He also had seven sons and three daughters. And he called the name of the first Jemimah, the name of the second Keziah, and the name of the third Keren-Happuch. In all the land were found no women so beautiful as the daughters of Job; and their father gave them an inheritance among their brothers.
>
> After this Job lived one hundred and forty years, and saw his children and grandchildren for four generations. So Job died, old and full of days.

Hezekiah's Life-Giving Tears

King Hezekiah's life also demonstrates the power of tears to express the sound of now and lead to miracle breakthrough.

Hezekiah walked with God and "did what was good and right and true before the LORD his God" (2 Chronicles 31:20). In fact, the Bible makes the distinction that Hezekiah trusted in the Lord so much that there was no other king of Judah after him or before him who could compare to him. Still, he faced premature death.

Let's listen in to the story: "In those days Hezekiah was sick and near death. And Isaiah the prophet, the son of Amoz, went to him and said to him, 'Thus says the LORD: "Set your house in order, for you shall die, and not live"'" (2 Kings 20:1).

Let's stop right there. Can you imagine a prophet—and not just any prophet but the prophet Isaiah—prophesying your imminent death? Isaiah's words carried weight. It must have seemed like a sure death sentence. But Hezekiah did not give up in the face of what sounded like an impossible fate:

> Then he turned his face toward the wall, and prayed to the LORD, saying, "Remember now, O LORD, I pray, how I have walked before You in truth and with a loyal heart, and have done what was good in Your sight." And Hezekiah wept bitterly.
>
> 2 Kings 20:2–3

Hezekiah did not just shed a few tears. He prayed with desperation. He knew the outcome had nothing to do with him or how eloquently he prayed. He was utterly dependent on God. Watch what happens next:

> And it happened, before Isaiah had gone out into the middle court, that the word of the LORD came to him, saying, "Return and tell Hezekiah the leader of My people, 'Thus says the LORD, the God of David your father: "I have heard your

prayer, I have seen your tears; surely I will heal you. On the third day you shall go up to the house of the LORD. And I will add to your days fifteen years. I will deliver you and this city from the hand of the king of Assyria; and I will defend this city for My own sake, and for the sake of My servant David."'"

Then Isaiah said, "Take a lump of figs." So they took and laid it on the boil, and he recovered.

2 Kings 20:4–7

That was a 24-hour breakthrough, which we will look at in the next chapter. Whatever you are facing, never give up. If all you can do is weep bitterly, then weep. Remember, when we come to the end of ourselves, we set ourselves up for a miracle we could never make happen in our own strength. One day, there will be no more tears, and we will live in perpetual breakthrough.

Revelation 21:4 promises this: "God will wipe away every tear from their eyes; there shall be no more death, nor sorrow, nor crying. There shall be no more pain, for the former things have passed away." Revelation 7:17 assures us, "The Lamb who is in the midst of the throne will shepherd them and lead them to living fountains of waters. And God will wipe away every tear from their eyes."

14

When to Expect Answers to the Sound of Now

It has been said that God moves in mysterious ways, but when you have a revelation of the ways of God, your faith soars. One of the mysteries of God is how He moves in and out of time. Elohim, Creator God, is the creator of time and is not subject to time. He can, therefore, deliver a breakthrough right on time.

Surely you have heard it said by someone that God is never late. The God of time who steps into our timeline to bring His will to pass in our lives in response to our desperate prayer is always right on time. He may show up at 11:59 p.m. when your faith is hanging by a thread, but the sound of now you release in a moment of pure desperation lingers in His ears, and He will not disappoint.

The sound of now does not always bring a now answer. But sometimes it does. The sound of now can manifest immediately—within 24 hours—or suddenly—after a couple of days or sometimes longer.

An *immediately* means just what its name implies: As soon as you release the sound of now, your answer comes instantly; there is no delay. A *24-hour breakthrough* is also literal: The answer you seek comes within 24 hours of your prayer. A *suddenly* is an answer that comes sometime later, and it comes unexpectedly and without warning.

Our faith is not in our sound; our faith is in the right-now God who hears us when we pray according to His will.

Immediatelies

The quickest of the Lord's answers to the sound of now is immediately. We see the concept of "immediatelies" well over a hundred times in Scripture. The gospel of Matthew gives us a vivid picture of Jesus' reaching out without delay to a cry for help.

Peter had just done the impossible. He had walked on water until he let his natural sight overtake his spiritual sight, and fear overtook him. But Peter did not give up and sink to the bottom of the sea. No, he released the sound of now: "Beginning to sink he cried out, saying, 'Lord, save me!' And immediately Jesus stretched out His hand and caught him" (Matthew 14:30–31).

Jesus did not wait until Peter was lost in the waves. He responded immediately to the cry, even though the cry was mixed with fear. Let that encourage you to keep crying out even when fear and unbelief are bombarding your mind in what appears to be an impossible circumstance.

Quite often in Scripture the immediate answer to prayer involves some form of healing. In one familiar story, we see a great multitude following Jesus. Imagine all the noise! But a single leper came to him and released the sound of now: "And behold, a leper came and worshiped Him, saying, 'Lord, if You are willing, You can make me clean.' Then Jesus put out His hand and touched him, saying, 'I am willing; be cleansed.' Immediately his leprosy was cleansed" (Matthew 8:2–3).

Think about this encounter beyond the context of healing. One minute this man was an outcast, rejected, in pain and with no hope for the future. He released the sound of now through worship and prayer, and immediately his life changed completely. Immediately, he had a brand-new lease on life. Immediately.

In another story, two blind men were sitting by the side of the road while Jesus walked by. They could not see Him, but that did not stop them from releasing the sound of now. The Bible says they cried out for mercy and prayed for their eyes to be opened. "So Jesus had compassion and touched their eyes. And immediately their eyes received sight, and they followed Him" (Matthew 20:34).

Remember, God is the one who chooses when to move immediately. Although your prayer touches His heart immediately, His perfect timing brings the answer at just the right time. Meaning, sometimes He waits.

24-Hour Breakthroughs

As I wrote in the first chapter, I was on the way to church when I saw a truck with the lettering *The Sound of Now* on its side. The words were glowing with glory in the Spirit.

I asked the Lord, "What is the sound of now?"

He said, *Faith is now.*

By the time I got to church, I had a full download. The Holy Spirit told me to prophesy a "24-hour breakthrough."

At the time, that was a pretty bold move for me. I do not typically prophesy dates and times, and I had never prophesied a 24-hour breakthrough. I mean, you had better be sure you are hearing from God if you are going to prophesy a 24-hour breakthrough!

The resultant breakthroughs started immediately. (You can watch that "sound of now" service at ahop.online.) Many people felt oppression lift. A young woman was delivered from hopelessness and a spirit of death. As I spoke life over her, she began to convulse and groan until she seemed lifeless on the floor. I never laid a hand on her. It was a breakthrough atmosphere created by the sound of now.

So many breakthrough testimonies flooded in from that 24 hours that we held a testimony service the following week. One of my favorite testimonies was from a young man who had a desire to play college football but was running out of hope. He was about to graduate from high school and still had no college prospects. His coach told him he should give up, but he had faith in his heart. He sowed the only five dollars he had into the offering and cried out to God for a breakthrough. The next day, he received a full scholarship to an Ivy League school.

I received three 24-hour breakthroughs in my own life. While I was preaching the message on the sound of now, I received a voicemail recording on my phone that I listened to the next day. The call was from someone in a major television producer's office asking me to work on a special project.

Before I could finish rejoicing over that offer, I got an email message from a former executive at a major media company asking me if I needed help in my media business. You have to understand: I was in sore need of an editor to help with *Awakening Magazine* and *365 Prophetic*, an online magazine with articles that inspire you to live a prophetic lifestyle. I had interviewed many candidates only to be disappointed and set back further on my schedule. I was stymied and stalled and stressed without enough help, but I kept pressing on to fulfill the prophetic words spoken over my life to take up the mantle of ministry through various media. This was an answer to prayer!

Then I received a text from someone in my family who had been unreachable for a while. I had been praying that this person would emerge and stop running from God. The text was an apology and an invitation to get together. That was breakthrough.

I looked at the clock and the three breakthroughs took place right within the 24-hour window.

A good biblical example of a literal 24-hour breakthrough is the time Elisha prophesied an end to famine, just as Elijah had prophesied an end to drought years before him.

Samaria, the capital of Israel, the Northern Kingdom, was being besieged by the Syrians, and there was a great famine in the city. But Elisha prophesied this: "Hear the word of the LORD. Thus says the LORD: 'Tomorrow about this time a seah of fine flour shall be sold for a shekel, and two seahs of barley for a shekel, at the gate of Samaria'" (2 Kings 7:1).

Not everyone believed Elisha, but it happened in an unpredictable way. Four lepers were sitting at the city gate, outcasts of society. They started talking among themselves and concluded that if they sat where they were they would starve, and if they sought shelter within the city of Samaria they would starve. So they decided to go to the camp of the Syrians, who did not have such strict laws about lepers, and surrender. If they were spared, the four would live; if the Syrians killed them, they were about to die anyway.

As it turns out, the Lord had caused the Syrian army to hear the noise of chariots, horses and a great army—and it had fled. When the lepers entered the camp, they found that they had hit the jackpot of loot. There were horses, donkeys, food, silver, gold, clothing. After deliberating whether they should keep the breakthrough to themselves or share it, they decided to let Israel's king know.

Elisha's prophecy came true, and Israel experienced a 24-hour breakthrough.

Our times are in God's hands (see Psalm 31:15). If the Lord has given a promise to you, hold on to it; He will bring it to pass. Sometimes answers come immediately. Sometimes breakthroughs come in rapid-fire succession in 24 hours. But sometimes the sound of now penetrates the darkness only after a long season of war. I prefer an immediately or a 24-hour breakthrough, and probably you do, too. But sometimes days keep passing, and the answer seems no closer. Maybe you have a decision to make and cannot discern God's will. Maybe you are seeking healing for a loved one and are growing weary in prayer.

If this is the case with you, it is time to strengthen yourself in prayer. Begin to release the sound that says, "Now I want my blessing. Now I want my breakthrough. Now I want everything Jesus died to give me. Now I want to see the manifestation of my healing Jesus paid for on the cross by His stripes. Now I want to see my prodigal come home. Now I want to see my finances increase. Now I want to see that promotion that was robbed from me. Now I want to walk in the promises of God. Now!"

Continue to cry out in faith. Your sound of now will move Jesus with compassion and position you to receive the final type of answered prayer: a suddenly.

Suddenlies

Over the years, I have heard a lot of prophecies about "suddenlies." You probably have, too! And I have prophesied suddenlies myself. We know God is a God of suddenlies. Just as the wind can suddenly blow, God can suddenly breathe on a difficult situation. When it seems He is nowhere to be found, He shows up suddenly. When all seems silent, He speaks suddenly. When all looks lost, He does miracles suddenly.

The dictionary definition of *suddenly* is "happening or coming unexpectedly; changing an angle or character all at once; marking or manifesting abruptness or haste; made or brought about in a short time."

We read about these unexpected happenings, changing angles and sudden shifts throughout the pages of Scripture. Perhaps the most famous account occurred shortly after the risen Christ spent forty days teaching His disciples about the Kingdom of God. After Jesus concluded His intensive ministry to them, He told the disciples not to leave Jerusalem, but to wait for the Holy Spirit He had been promising them. Jesus was taken up into a cloud, and they went to Jerusalem to wait for the promise.

While they were waiting—120 altogether—they were not gossiping about the Pharisees. They were not complaining about how long it was taking to receive the promise of the Holy Spirit. They were not debating about who would be the greatest among them. No, the Bible tells us exactly what they were doing: "These all continued with one accord in prayer and supplication, with the women and Mary the mother of Jesus, and with His brothers" (Acts 1:14).

Still, nothing happened. As the days passed, the disciples were not weary in well doing. They were not losing hope in the promise. They were waiting with expectation and faith.

Note also in this story an unfailing principle of releasing the sound of now: "They were all with one accord in one place" (Acts 2:1). In other words, they were releasing the sound of unified prayer, a sound heaven could not ignore. This kind of unity means no double-mindedness. It means praying and praising with sincerity despite how bad it looks. We know that where there is unity, God commands a blessing (see Psalm 133:1–2). And what happened as a result of their unified prayer was no small blessing.

Let's look at this scene in the Upper Room in context:

> When the Day of Pentecost had fully come, they were all with one accord in one place. And suddenly there came a sound from heaven, as of a rushing mighty wind, and it filled the whole house where they were sitting. Then there appeared to them divided tongues, as of fire, and one sat upon each of them. And they were all filled with the Holy Spirit and began to speak with other tongues, as the Spirit gave them utterance.
>
> Acts 2:1–4

The 120 disciples had spent days in prayer, and then suddenly the Holy Spirit moved—He shook the place and filled them. They never forgot it.

In Isaiah 48:3, God says, "I have declared the former things from the beginning; they went forth from My mouth, and I caused them to hear it. Suddenly I did them, and they came to pass." Maybe you need a suddenly in your life. You need a sudden shift into a job promotion or a sudden shift from sickness to divine health. God can shift you into greater authority in the spirit—suddenly. He can move you out of that desperate dark night of the soul to a season of intimacy and revelation such as you have never experienced before—suddenly. Suddenly, you move from oppression to a level of freedom you did not know existed. Suddenly.

Keep on Till One or the Other Happens

You might release the sound of now, and the miracle comes even as you declare your amen. But if the answer seems slow in appearing, keep declaring the sound of now. Maybe you need a job, but no one is hiring, or you need to find a new place to live, and landlords keep rejecting you, and you are running out of time. Release the sound of now to invite Jesus into your situation and watch what happens. You can be right in the middle of God's will and still face storms, but God can deliver you.

Let this passage build your faith:

> Now when evening came, His disciples went down to the sea, got into the boat, and went over the sea toward Capernaum. And it was already dark, and Jesus had not come to them. Then the sea arose because a great wind was blowing. So when they had rowed about three or four miles, they saw Jesus walking on the sea and drawing near the boat; and they were afraid. But He said to them, "It is I; do not be afraid." Then they willingly received Him into the boat, and immediately the boat was at the land where they were going.
>
> John 6:16–21

Storms may be raging all around you, but it is up to you what spiritual climate you create. Only you can release the sound of now that invites the Holy Spirit to work in your heart, in your life and in your circumstances. We will talk more about persevering until something happens in the next chapter.

15

When the Sound of Now Is Persistence

One day a farmer's donkey fell into a dry well. The farmer scratched his head trying to come up with a way to rescue the poor creature. Finally, he decided it was just impossible. The animal was old, and sadly, there was nothing he could do. So the farmer asked his neighbors to come over and help him cover up the well. They all grabbed shovels and began to shovel dirt into the well.

At first, the donkey continued his loud braying, but then he quieted down and let out some contented sounds. The farmer looked down the well to see what was happening: With every shovel of dirt that fell upon him, the donkey shook it off and took a step up.

Now, with new motivation, the farmer and his neighbors continued to shovel dirt. The donkey would shake it off and take a step up. Pretty soon, the donkey stepped out of the well and trotted off!

Moral: Life is going to shovel dirt on you. The trick to surviving is to shake off the dirt and take a step up. Every adversity can be used if you refuse to give up. Shake yourself off and take a step up.

In other words, what happens to you is not nearly as important as how you react to it.

This is not my story; it is a fable that has been repeated far and wide, but it seemed appropriate to tell again in this context. You have also heard it said that persistence pays off. My life proves it. I always say the best thing I have going for me is that I refuse to quit. I have had lots of dirt dumped on my head. Life has thrown me at least my fair share of curve balls, but my testimony is this: "I'm still here. And I am walking in my prophetic destiny."

For all the miracle breakthroughs I have experienced and witnessed after releasing the sound of now, I would be remiss not to help you understand that the sound of now does not always drive instant results. Sometimes the sound of now demands perseverance and persistence. The enemy is a resister. He tries to wear us out and wear us down. That is why Paul, inspired by the Holy Spirit, wrote, "Let us not grow weary while doing good, for in due season we shall reap if we do not lose heart" (Galatians 6:9), and, "But as for you, brethren, do not grow weary in doing good" (2 Thessalonians 3:13). Let these stories encourage you.

A Persistent Widow

Jesus taught His disciples that they should always pray and never give up. When we do not feel like praying, it is a sure sign that the enemy has attacked our hope. If he can hinder our hope, he can hamper our faith, because faith is the substance of things hoped for (see Hebrews 11:1). Hope is a necessary ingredient of faith. To illustrate the point, Jesus told His disciples a story:

> "In a certain town there was a civil judge, a thick-skinned and godless man who had no fear of others' opinions. And there was a poor widow in that town who kept pleading with the judge, 'Grant me justice and protect me against my oppressor!'
>
> "He ignored her pleas for quite some time, but she kept asking. Eventually he said to himself, 'This widow keeps annoying me, demanding her rights, and I'm tired of listening to her. Even though I'm not a religious man and don't care about the opinions of others, I'll just get her off my back by answering her claims for justice and I'll rule in her favor. Then she'll leave me alone.'"
>
> The Lord continued, "Did you hear what the ungodly judge said—that he would answer her persistent request? Don't you know that God, the true judge, will grant justice to all of his chosen ones who cry out to him night and day? He will pour out his Spirit upon them. He will not delay to answer you and give you what you ask for. God will give swift justice to those who don't give up. So be ever praying, ever expecting, just like the widow was with the judge. Yet when the Son of Man comes back, will he find this kind of persistent faithfulness in his people?"
>
> Luke 18:2–8 TPT

You may not be a poor widow, but you can probably relate to releasing petitions, supplications and all manner of prayer, and then feeling as if God is ignoring you—or at least not answering you. Although this parable speaks about a woman seeking justice, the principle of persistence applies to any prayer campaign for breakthrough.

Sometimes your breakthrough is the sound of perseverance. Sometimes perseverance is displayed through continual prayer, that bulldog tenacity that refuses to quit. Sometimes we really have to "pray without ceasing" (1 Thessalonians 5:17). So be ever praying, ever expecting, just as the widow was with the judge. Your persistence produces the sound of now that will break that miracle barrier in time.

A Persistent Neighbor

When Jesus' disciples ask Him to teach them how to pray, He started with the model prayer that we call the Lord's Prayer. But Jesus did not stop there. He went on to give an illustration of persistent prayer:

> And He said to them, "Which of you shall have a friend, and go to him at midnight and say to him, 'Friend, lend me three loaves; for a friend of mine has come to me on his journey, and I have nothing to set before him'; and he will answer from within and say, 'Do not trouble me; the door is now shut, and my children are with me in bed; I cannot rise and give to you'? I say to you, though he will not rise and give to him because he is his friend, yet because of his persistence he will rise and give him as many as he needs.
>
> "So I say to you, ask, and it will be given to you; seek, and you will find; knock, and it will be opened to you. For everyone who asks receives, and he who seeks finds, and to him who knocks it will be opened. If a son asks for bread from any father among you, will he give him a stone? Or if he asks for a fish, will he give him a serpent instead of a fish? Or if he asks for an egg, will he offer him a scorpion? If you then, being evil, know how to give good gifts to your

children, how much more will your heavenly Father give the Holy Spirit to those who ask Him!"

Luke 11:5–13

Catch that. The man did not open the door out of friend-ship but out of persistence. Noteworthy is the *Amplified Bible, Classic Edition*, translation of Luke 11:9: "Ask and keep on asking and it shall be given you; seek and keep on seeking and you shall find; knock and keep on knocking and the door shall be opened to you."

I like this translation because it expounds upon the persis-tence that is sometimes necessary in order to see the break-through. Persistence has a sound that accumulates over time until it penetrates the obstacles blocking your miracle.

Paul revealed one of the secrets of his success in Philippi-ans 3:14: "I press toward the goal for the prize of the upward call of God in Christ Jesus." And the writer of Hebrews let us know that "you have need of endurance, so that after you have done the will of God, you may receive the promise" (Hebrews 10:36).

Releasing Pent-Up Promises

Many people give up right at the edge of breakthrough. Many people fail to press all the way through and wind up dis-appointed and disillusioned. They lose it before it is com-pletely manifested.

The enemy will not give up until you push him all the way back. Keep on making the sound of now through your persis-tence. Keep pressing until the breakthrough is in your hand.

The business world regards something called a "pent-up demand." This refers to an especially strong demand by the public for a particular product. If there is a pent-up demand in your heart, a prayer that you have been holding with persistence, keep on releasing the sound of now and position yourself for the miracle breakthrough that many others have already received. It is up to you to put a demand on the Word of God to manifest now. It is up to you to put a demand on the anointing that abides within you to break yokes that are oppressing you. It is up to you to put a demand on the promise of answered prayer and say, "*Now!*"

We are not supposed to be sick and poor and tired. There is Christian suffering and tribulation, meaning there is opposition to our work for the Kingdom, but we are not called to suffer sickness and defeat and lack at the whim of the enemy. The sound of now is aggressive. Let this be your confession:

I receive my provision now.

I receive my healing now.

I receive my breakthrough now.

I receive my promotion now.

I receive the revelation that will set me free now.

I receive my deliverance now.

I receive the demonstration of power in my life now.

I receive the ability to move in signs and wonders and miracles so people can see that Jesus is alive—now.

When I prophesied a 24-hour breakthrough that Sunday morning, I had a vision. It looked as if promises that had been put into a corked bottle were being loosed. If your prayers and tears regarding a promise are in a bottle, know that God will pop the cork. You will experience a champagne celebration where the promises shoot out of the bottle top with explosive force. I prophesy an eruption of breakthrough in your life!

16

Releasing the Sound of Now in Intercession

When Rees Howells, the great Welsh intercessor, heard sounds of doom transmitting from his radio—the voice of newscasters describing Nazi movement toward Great Britain during World War II—he did not let fear grip his heart. Instead, he released the sound of now. It was a desperate sound of faith as a Nazi invasion of Britain seemed imminent.

Howells's stance is recorded in his diary on May 18, 1940: "We are here until these Nazis are put out."[1] His diary also records his desperation in intercession: "Unless God intervenes today in a miraculous way, I believe we have lost. I would be willing to die, but I cannot afford to die, neither can we afford that Hitler should live."[2]

Later that same day, he demonstrated his determination with these words in his journal: "I want to fight with this enemy again this weekend as if it were the end of civilization. You don't leave anything to chance in this."[3] Although we cannot hear his actual prayers, we can hear the sound of now as expressed in his biography, *Rees Howells, Intercessor*.

Rees led a company of intercessors in desperate, determined faith to produce a sound that reached heaven. At that moment, hundreds of thousands of British and other Allied troops were becoming trapped on the beaches of Dunkirk, a small coastal town in north France. Advancing German forces were poised to wipe them out. Their only hope was evacuation and transport across the channel to England.

In what history records as the "Miracle of Dunkirk," unexplainably, Adolf Hitler gave a temporary halt order to the armored columns bearing down on the soldiers, allowing Allied command crucial time to plan an evacuation. From May 26 to June 4, 1940, more than 338,000 men were rescued in Operation Dynamo, a turning point in the war, and surely an answer to the sound of now in intercession.

There are crises that demand the sound of now to push one's prayers past the principalities warring in the heavens trying to defeat God's will. This story teaches us that the sound of now is imperative not only for our personal concerns but also for the needs of others. The sound of now in intercession can help other people, companies, cities, even nations experience the breakthrough that otherwise eludes them.

When Intercession Is Action

Although intercession correlates directly with prayer, not all intercession is prayer. Sometimes the sound of now is expressed through a faith-inspired action. After all, faith without works is dead (see James 2:26). Works based on faith have a sound in the spirit that our natural ears do not perceive but God's ears hear clearly.

The Hebrew word for *intercession* is *paga*. According to *Brown, Driver, Briggs Hebrew Lexicon*, it means not only "to pray," but also "to meet, touch, strike and reach the mark." The dictionary adds that *intercession* is an "intervening between two parties with a view to reconcile differences." Intercession is more than prayer, though it includes prayer.

The Bible gives us many examples of faith in action— and in the case of the friends of the paraplegic man, urgent action:

> One day many Jewish religious leaders, known as Pharisees along with many religious scholars came from every village of Galilee, throughout Judea, and even from Jerusalem to hear Jesus teach. And the power of the Lord God surged through him to instantly heal.
>
> Some men came to Jesus, carrying a paraplegic man on a stretcher. They attempted to bring him in past the crowd to set him down in front of Jesus. But because there were so many people crowding the door, they had no way to bring him inside. So they crawled onto the roof, dug their way through the roof tiles, and lowered the man, stretcher and all, into the middle of the crowd, right in front of Jesus.
>
> Seeing the demonstration of their faith, Jesus said to the paraplegic man, "My friend, your sins are forgiven!"
>
> Luke 5:17–20 TPT

The paraplegic's friends did not know if, at any moment, Jesus might cease His ministry and withdraw to a mountain to pray. They were determined to get their friend the help he needed while they had the chance—now. The sound of now is an urgent sound that is sometimes expressed through unusual acts of intercession. It comes from a heart determined to do whatever it takes to position itself for a breakthrough.

When Intercession Is Risky Business

Sometimes intercession is risky business. Let's look again at the story of Queen Esther. There is no record of any particular intercessory prayer she released to Jehovah God when Haman was plotting to destroy the Jews. Though she may have prayed plenty, the Bible does not give us any idea what petitions she lifted up. What we do see is her intercession in action.

As the chronicle goes, there was great mourning among the Jews when King Ahasuerus agreed to Haman's request to issue a decree that they should be destroyed. When Esther's maids and eunuchs told her that her uncle, Mordecai, was wearing sackcloth, a symbol of mourning, she was deeply distressed (see Esther 4:4). Sometimes, that is where the sound of now begins—in our deep distress. Although Esther sent clothes to her uncle, he would not remove the garments of mourning. What he did instead was send Esther a copy of the king's fateful decree hoping she would make a plea to her husband on behalf of her people. King Ahasuerus did not know that his wife was a Jew.

This kind of intercession was dangerous. First of all, a decree cannot be "undecreed"—you cannot unring that bell. Secondly, it was law that anyone who entered the king's inner court without being summoned would meet with the reality of another decree—a death sentence—unless the king extended the golden scepter (see Esther 4:11). The scepter was a symbol of royal authority and spoke of protection or punishment. Thanks be to God that through Jesus Christ He has extended His rod of authority, and we are invited to into the inner court where our pleas are heard!

When Esther's reluctance to risk her life in an act of intercession for the Jews got back to Mordecai, he pressed her with these harrowing words:

Releasing the Sound of Now in Intercession

"Do not think in your heart that you will escape in the king's palace any more than all the other Jews. For if you remain completely silent at this time, relief and deliverance will arise for the Jews from another place, but you and your father's house will perish. Yet who knows whether you have come to the kingdom for such a time as this?"

Esther 4:13–14

Esther got the revelation and responded, "If I perish, I perish."

This is the heart posture of an intercessor releasing the sound of now. Esther found favor in the king's sight. He invited her to make a request, promising her up to half the kingdom. Ultimately, Hamon's conspiracy failed because of Esther's sound of now. Haman was hanged on the gallows he had intended to use for Mordecai, and King Ahasuerus issued a second decree that allowed the Jews to take up arms and defend themselves. The Jews prevailed because Esther stood in the gap despite her own peril.

Standing in the Gap

One of the saddest verses in the Bible is Ezekiel 22:30, where God says: "I sought for a man among them who would make a wall, and stand in the gap before Me on behalf of the land, that I should not destroy it; but I found no one." Destruction can come as a result of the lack of intercession. The good news is the sound of now in intercession can change everything.

Abraham and Moses—two mighty intercessors—also released the sound of now that saved lives.

Consider the scene after Moses came down from the mountain, holding the stone tablets with the Ten Commandments carved into them. The Israelites had given up on Moses and wanted Aaron, God's chosen high priest, to make new gods for them. Aaron complied and constructed a golden calf, which they began to worship, but God knew what they had done:

> And the LORD said to Moses, "I have seen this people, and indeed it is a stiff-necked people! Now therefore, let Me alone, that My wrath may burn hot against them and I may consume them. And I will make of you a great nation."
>
> Exodus 32:9–10

This was probably tempting to Moses, who was also upset with the Israelites. But Moses did not take God up on His offer. Instead, he released the sound of now in intercession, which sounds like reasoning together with God (see Isaiah 1:18):

> Then Moses pleaded with the LORD his God, and said: "LORD, why does Your wrath burn hot against Your people whom You have brought out of the land of Egypt with great power and with a mighty hand? Why should the Egyptians speak, and say, 'He brought them out to harm them, to kill them in the mountains, and to consume them from the face of the earth'? Turn from Your fierce wrath, and relent from this harm to Your people. Remember Abraham, Isaac, and Israel, Your servants, to whom You swore by Your own self, and said to them, 'I will multiply your descendants as the stars of heaven; and all this land that I have spoken of I give to your descendants, and they shall inherit it forever.'" So the LORD relented from the harm which He said He would do to His people.
>
> Exodus 32:11–14

Abraham also stood in the gap with a sound. God was going down to Sodom and Gomorrah because He had heard the outcry against the wicked city. Along with Abraham, we get to listen in on a conversation in heaven: "And the LORD said, 'Shall I hide from Abraham what I am doing, since Abraham shall surely become a great and mighty nation, and all the nations of the earth shall be blessed in him?'" (Genesis 18:17–18). God did not hide his intentions from Abraham because He wanted Abraham to intercede for the righteous in the city and knew he would. Read the dramatic account of Abraham releasing the sound of now in intercession:

Abraham still stood before the LORD. And Abraham came near and said, "Would You also destroy the righteous with the wicked? Suppose there were fifty righteous within the city; would You also destroy the place and not spare it for the fifty righteous that were in it? Far be it from You to do such a thing as this, to slay the righteous with the wicked, so that the righteous should be as the wicked; far be it from You! Shall not the Judge of all the earth do right?"

So the LORD said, "If I find in Sodom fifty righteous within the city, then I will spare all the place for their sakes."

Then Abraham answered and said, "Indeed now, I who am but dust and ashes have taken it upon myself to speak to the Lord: Suppose there were five less than the fifty righteous; would You destroy all of the city for lack of five?"

So He said, "If I find there forty-five, I will not destroy it."

And he spoke to Him yet again and said, "Suppose there should be forty found there?"

So He said, "I will not do it for the sake of forty."

Then he said, "Let not the Lord be angry, and I will speak: Suppose thirty should be found there?"

So He said, "I will not do it if I find thirty there."

And he said, "Indeed now, I have taken it upon myself to speak to the Lord: Suppose twenty should be found there?"

So He said, "I will not destroy it for the sake of twenty."

Then he said, "Let not the Lord be angry, and I will speak but once more: Suppose ten should be found there?"

And He said, "I will not destroy it for the sake of ten." So the Lord went His way as soon as He had finished speaking with Abraham; and Abraham returned to his place.

Genesis 18:22–33

The end of the story: Ten could not be found, but the only righteous people in the city, Lot and his immediate family, were rescued before fire and brimstone fell.

Practical Intercession

The Bible commands us to pray for others. Paul exhorts us to make supplications, prayers, intercessions and thanksgiving for all people, and notably those who are in authority (see 1 Timothy 2:1). We are even supposed to pray for those who persecute us (see Matthew 5:44). So how do we intercede, in practical terms, in the context of the sound of now in intercession?

Releasing the sound of now in intercession starts with being touched by the need of another. When you truly feel the urgency, the pain, the sorrow of the one for whom you are making intercession, you position yourself like Christ, who is seated in heavenly places even now making intercession for us.

Christ is the ultimate intercessor, in part because He understands what we are going through. The writer of Hebrews encourages us in this regard:

Seeing then that we have a great High Priest who has passed through the heavens, Jesus the Son of God, let us hold fast our confession. For we do not have a High Priest who cannot sympathize with our weaknesses, but was in all points tempted as we are, yet without sin.

Hebrews 4:14–15

When you take on this feeling of the suffering or the need of another, it is because God Himself has given you a prayer burden. He is assigning you to help that person carry the burden in prayer. Once you feel the burden, the next step is to agree with the need.

Agreement in itself makes a certain sound. We know this is true when individuals pray together in unity. Matthew 18:19 tells us that if any two on earth agree about anything, it will be done. The *Amplified Bible, Classic Edition*'s version of this verse helps illustrate the sound of now: "Again I tell you, if two of you on earth agree (harmonize together, make a symphony together) about whatever [anything and everything] they may ask, it will come to pass and be done for them by My Father in heaven."

When you have this harmony—not only when you are with like-minded intercessors, but also when you feel a burden and agree with the need—you can pray God's Word with confidence. God's Word never fails and never returns void.

The final ingredient in the basic recipe for releasing the sound of now in intercession is consistency. Consistency in prayer also has a sound. It is the sound of determination. It is the sound of desperation. It is the sound of faith that will not give up. *It is the sound of now.* Some battles require a single prayer, and others require long-term intercession.

149

Remember, the Lord always answers the sound of now that comes through desperate cries. Never grow weary in doing good, because you will reap the prayer answers if you do not give up.

17

Many Manifestations of the Sound of Now

Although we only have one voice, linguistic experts reveal that humans can make hundreds of distinct sounds. By way of comparison, although there is only one sound of now, it can be expressed in many different ways. Indeed, as I pored through Scriptures searching for sounds of now, I discovered there are too many to explore in depth in a single book.

I thought it was important, though—if only for the sake of demonstrating that there may be a way you release the sound that we have not covered—to relay a few more scriptural examples. Surely, there are sounds of now I have not discovered yet—but maybe you will.

Now Sounds That Release Blessing

Let's start with one you are undoubtedly familiar with. It is found in 1 Chronicles. It is a sound that unlocks blessing, increase and favor. This sound is found in the prayer of Jabez:

Now Jabez was more honorable than his brothers, and his mother called his name Jabez, saying, "Because I bore him in hardship." Then Jabez called on the God of Israel, saying, "Oh, that You would indeed bless me and enlarge my territory, that Your hand might be with me, and that You would keep me from evil, that it may not bring me hardship!" So God granted what he asked.

1 Chronicles 4:9–10 MEV

Can you hear the sound of now in this? It is a sound of desperate faith coming from the heart of one whose name means "sorrowful." Jabez was a son of Judah. That makes him a son of praise, since Judah is the tribe known for praise. But in his birth Jabez caused pain, and his mother named him for the pain he caused. Now consider this: In ancient Israeli culture, your name was a big deal. Jabez was set up for failure, marked as one who causes pain. It would be like your parents naming you Disaster or Problematic.

Every time people called Jabez's name, they were declaring that he caused sorrow. He heard his whole life about how he caused sorrow. He had to overcome this stigma of causing pain. Jabez called on the Lord God to reverse his lot in life—and God answered his prayer.

The sound of now releases blessing. No matter what disadvantage you have in life, you can overcome it with a sound of now that unlocks favor, increase and power.

Now Sounds That Release Revival

There is a sound of now that unlocks revival. Let's look once more at this powerful passage:

> When the Day of Pentecost had fully come, they were all with one accord in one place. And suddenly there came a sound from heaven, as of a rushing mighty wind, and it filled the whole house where they were sitting. Then there appeared to them divided tongues, as of fire, and one sat upon each of them. And they were all filled with the Holy Spirit and began to speak with other tongues, as the Spirit gave them utterance.
>
> Acts 2:1–4

This sound not only launched the New Testament Church, but it had a ripple effect. The sound of the Holy Spirit led to the sound of tongues, followed by the sound of a bold Gospel presentation and ultimately the sound of revival. Scripture tells us the result of the Holy Spirit's movement:

> Then those who gladly received his word were baptized; and that day about three thousand souls were added to them. And they continued steadfastly in the apostles' doctrine and fellowship, in the breaking of bread, and in prayers. Then fear came upon every soul, and many wonders and signs were done through the apostles. Now all who believed were together, and had all things in common, and sold their possessions and goods, and divided them among all, as anyone had need.
>
> Acts 2:41–45

While some mark *revival* as simply a transitory, goosebump experience or a "good meeting," the sound of now will break through the four walls of the Church to reach the lost.

Now Sounds That Release God's Glory

There is a sound of now that releases glory. Moses released this sound through a prayer that moved God's heart. Moses was known to meet with the Lord in a place accurately called the "Tabernacle of meeting." When Moses entered the Tabernacle, "the pillar of cloud descended and stood at the door . . . and the LORD talked with Moses . . . face to face, as a man speaks to his friend" (Exodus 33:9, 11).

In one particular dialogue, Moses asked the Lord to assure him that, if indeed he had found grace in His sight, God would show Moses His way to lead His people. The Lord promised Moses that His presence would go with him and that He would give the prophet rest.

At the end of their meeting, Moses asked boldly, "Please, show me Your glory" (Exodus 33:18). God was not obliged to show Moses His glory, but the meek prophet's heartfelt petition—the petition from a friend—compelled the Lord to answer:

> "I will make all My goodness pass before you, and I will proclaim the name of the LORD before you. I will be gracious to whom I will be gracious, and I will have compassion on whom I will have compassion." But He said, "You cannot see My face; for no man shall see Me, and live." And the LORD said, "Here is a place by Me, and you shall stand on the rock. So it shall be, while My glory passes by, that I will put you in the cleft of the rock, and will cover you with My hand while I pass by. Then I will take away My hand, and you shall see My back; but My face shall not be seen."
>
> Exodus 33:19–23

Technically, we are all friends of God, though only a few in the Bible are named as such. Abraham, David and Moses are among them. There are realms God reserves for His friends. As such, we may sing out, "Show me Your glory," and release the sound of now that causes us to experience a measure of His glory.

Now Sounds That Attract God's Presence

There are certain sounds of now that attract God's presence, such as repentance, unity and praise.

In Peter's appeal to the Jews we find the concept of how repentance brings forth God's presence: "Now you must repent and turn back to God so that your sins will be removed, and so that times of refreshing will stream from the Lord's presence" (Acts 3:19 TPT). Peter also connected repentance with receiving the gift of the Holy Spirit (see Acts 2:38). Repentance implies drawing near to God, and we know when we draw near to Him He draws near to us (see James 4:8).

As we have noted, Scripture tells us that unity creates a heavenly harmony that draws God's blessings:

> How truly wonderful and delightful to see brothers and sisters living together in sweet unity! It's as precious as the sacred scented oil flowing from the head of the high priest Aaron, dripping down upon his beard and running all the way down to the hem of his priestly robes. This heavenly harmony can be compared to the dew dripping down from the skies upon Mount Hermon, refreshing the mountain slopes of Israel. For from this realm of sweet harmony God will release his eternal blessing, the promise of life forever!
>
> Psalm 133 TPT

We touched on praise as a sound of now, but it is worth mentioning from a different angle. There are sounds of now we create in praise that attract God's presence. And we know that God inhabits the praises of His people (see Psalm 22:3). The Passion Translation offers that verse in vivid words that illustrate the sound of now: "You are God-Enthroned, surrounded with songs, living among the shouts of praise of your princely people."

Not just any praise, spoken or sung, is a sound of now that attracts His presence. God is looking for those who will worship Him in spirit and in truth (see John 4:24).

Now Sounds That Release Vengeance

There is a sound of now that releases vengeance on the enemies of God. Remember, we are not wrestling against flesh and blood but against principalities, powers, rulers of the darkness and spiritual hosts of wickedness in high places (see Ephesians 6:12).

Samson, a mighty judge in Israel, released this sound after being deceived by Delilah, captured by the Philistines, blinded by the gouging out of his eyes, bound and pressed into forced labor, and ultimately made to perform like a circus animal:

> Then Samson called to the LORD, saying, "O Lord GOD, remember me, I pray! Strengthen me, I pray, just this once, O God, that I may with one blow take vengeance on the Philistines for my two eyes!" And Samson took hold of the two middle pillars which supported the temple, and he braced himself against them, one on his right and the other on his left. Then Samson said, "Let me die with the Philistines!" And he pushed with all his might, and the temple fell on the lords and all the people who were in it. So the dead that he killed at his death were more than he had killed in his life.
>
> Judges 16:28–30

Samson's prayer may seem selfish on the surface, but I believe his motive was to see enemies of God fall. Samson humbled himself in the face of his enemy's taunts and turned to God. In mocking Samson, they were effectively mocking God. And God shall not be mocked (see Galatians 6:7). Matthew Henry's *Commentary* offers this insight:

> Nothing fills up the sins of any person or people faster than mocking and misusing the servants of God, even though it is by their own folly that they are brought low. God put it into Samson's heart, as a public person, thus, to avenge on them God's quarrel, Israel's, and his own. That strength which he had lost by sin, he recovers by prayer. That it was not from passion or personal revenge, but from holy zeal for the glory of God and Israel, appears from God's accepting and answering the prayer. The house was pulled down, not by the natural strength of Samson, but by the almighty power of God.[1]

So remember, vengeance belongs to the Lord—and He will repay (see Romans 12:19). God will take vengeance on spirits that harass His people. When we forgive the people the enemy used to harm us, we can cry out as Samson did for God's vengeance to fall on the evil spirits.

Similarly, David cried out, "Lord God Almighty, you are the God who takes vengeance on your enemies. It's time for you to punish evil! Let your rays of revelation-light shine from your people and pierce the conscience of the wicked and punish them" (Psalm 94:1 TPT).

Now Sounds That Impede the Enemy's Plans

The sound of forgiveness is a sound of now that assures our own forgiveness—and puts up a powerful block against the enemy's efforts to disrupt our lives.

Think about it. If we will not forgive others, God will not forgive us (see Matthew 6:15). When we stand in anger

157

and unforgiveness, we come out from under God's hand of protection and, thereby, give place to the devil (see Ephesians 4:27). If you do not forgive, the enemy has a legal right to torment you.

When Peter asked Jesus how many times he might be expected to pardon a brother who sinned against him, making the magnanimous offer of seven times, Jesus replied that no limits were to be placed on the act of forgiveness.

Jesus went further and told him the story of the king who forgave a servant a large debt. That servant, in the familiar story recorded in Matthew 18:23–35, then refused to forgive a fellow servant a small debt and had the fellow servant thrown into prison. The king was angry with the first servant, rescinded his pardon and had him thrown in jail.

Jesus was clear: "So My heavenly Father also will do to you if each of you, from his heart, does not forgive his brother his trespasses" (Matthew 18:35).

Do you have someone you need to forgive?

18

Dealing with Backlash after Your Breakthrough

Elijah faced a monumental task—turning the heart of an idolatrous nation back to Jehovah. It was a big job and a lonely job. Most of the other prophets had fled Israel under the tyrannical rule of King Ahab or were massacred at Queen Jezebel's command. The rest of the prophets were either hiding in a cave eating bread and water or feasting at Jezebel's dinner table.

It is no wonder Elijah twice insisted, "I alone am left" (1 Kings 19:10, 14). He was on Ahab's hit list for prophesying the devastating drought and on Jezebel's most-wanted poster for killing her prophets at Mount Carmel.

Shortly before his words of fatalism, Elijah had seemed fearless, presenting himself to Ahab and calling for a prophetic showdown. He had challenged the wicked king to gather all Israel on Mount Carmel, along with the 450 false prophets who served Baal and the four hundred false prophets who served Jezebel. Ahab obliged, and Elijah got to work.

Elijah was up against popular opinion and demon powers, but he was a prophet on a mission. You know the story. The prophets of Baal tried tirelessly to get their false god to respond, but to no avail. The false prophets cried and jumped and cut themselves from morning to night in a useless effort to get an idol to move.

At the time of the evening sacrifice, Elijah repaired the altar, laid wood on it, commanded it to be drenched with water and said a simple prayer:

> And it came to pass, at the time of the offering of the evening sacrifice, that Elijah the prophet came near and said, "LORD God of Abraham, Isaac, and Israel, let it be known this day that You are God in Israel and I am Your servant, and that I have done all these things at Your word. Hear me, O LORD, hear me, that this people may know that You are the LORD God, and that You have turned their hearts back to You again."
>
> Then the fire of the LORD fell and consumed the burnt sacrifice, and the wood and the stones and the dust, and it licked up the water that was in the trench. Now when all the people saw it, they fell on their faces; and they said, "The LORD, He is God! The LORD, He is God!"
>
> 1 Kings 18:36–39

This was not just a breakthrough for Elijah; this was a breakthrough for a nation. Still, you can relate to his plight. Maybe you have been up against impossible odds, fighting for your marriage, battling cancer, praying for prodigals or trying to pay your overwhelming bills. Maybe you have released the sound of now in one of the many ways we have studied in this book.

And maybe you have received a monumental victory in your life as a result.

Here is what you need to remember now: After the breakthrough, there is often backlash. Backlash is the enemy's retaliation against your victory. The dictionary definition is telling: "a sudden violent backward movement or reaction; a strong adverse reaction."

My view on spiritual backlash comes from Newton's third law of motion: "For every action, there is an equal and opposite reaction." The enemy's backlash aims to cause you to abandon your breakthrough—or question if you ever had a real breakthrough at all.

When the Backlash Comes

Elijah's breakthrough was multifaceted and the backlash was immediate. Ahab went home and told Jezebel everything that happened. This would have been the perfect time for this evil regime to repent before the Lord, but Jezebel was outraged and sent a messenger to Elijah, threatening to kill him within 24 hours. That is the opposite of a 24-hour breakthrough!

The backlash in the spirit was so strong against Elijah that he ran for his life, left his servant behind at Beersheba, went a day's journey into the wilderness, sat under a broom tree and prayed that he might die (see 1 Kings 19:3–4). Then he slept and slept and slept. Then he traveled further, to Horeb, and hid in a cave like the fearful prophets he had set out to set free with his courageous showdown at Mount Carmel.

After one of the greatest breakthroughs in the Bible, we see a great hero give in to the enemy's backlash. I can only imagine that he was spiritually and emotionally exhausted— and sometimes so are we after a long battle for breakthrough.

We have wept, warred with a battle cry, shouted our lungs out, praised until our voices became hoarse and otherwise released sounds of desperate faith. The breakthrough came, and we let our guard down. But postbreakthrough is not the time to let your guard down.

I had a major battle with a false prophet who stole a book idea and plagiarized another book, publishing it and celebrating its success. This same false prophet was cursing me, splitting my church, meddling in marriages of those who worked for my ministry and otherwise causing problems. At the beginning of the Jezebel prophet's harassment, a prophetic friend of mine told me the battle would be over in about three months.

At about the three-month mark, things started to settle. We thought it was a fulfillment of the prophetic word until we got three separate, independent warnings from ministry friends who knew nothing at all about the situation. The gist of the warnings was this: Don't disregard what looks familiar; brace yourselves.

See, sometimes there is a calm before the enemy's next storm. We heeded the advance warning and braced for impact. We pushed back the darkness and sustained the false prophet's next blow. Our prophetic friend was ultimately right; the attack did end at the three-month mark; the last blow was backlash.

Keep in mind some backlash is immediate and some is not. Remember how Satan had finished tempting Jesus in the wilderness and had failed to move Him? The Bible tells us that the devil left Him until a more opportune time. When is an opportune time? Usually when we least expect it. I call it backlash. Do not be afraid of it; just take steps to maintain your breakthrough.

Bracing Yourself after the Breakthrough

When the dust settles on your breakthrough, you might not experience the measure of backlash Elijah saw. The enemy might not come with intimidating tactics or death threats; the attack may be subtler. But you will still have to maintain your breakthrough. After all, God called the serpent the most subtle creature in the garden (see Genesis 3:1).

As I did with the false prophet, you must brace yourself. One of my earliest prophetic mentors once told me this truth: "If you brace yourself for the hit, it will not do as much damage." The dictionary defines *bracing oneself* as "being prepared for something." Bracing yourself—or bracing up—is preparing yourself or readying yourself for the retaliation, the counterattack that will surely come.

Over the years I have seen the importance of following this advice. This is not a killjoy attitude to adopt; it is wisdom from above. You do not have to be paranoid, just alert. I am convinced most people who lose their breakthroughs were never taught to brace up, which is why I am stressing this point at the finale of this book.

If you get a breakthrough by landing a business partner or ministry collaboration, do not stop praying. The enemy can influence that individual to back out of the deal and leave you holding the bag. If you get a financial windfall that helps you pay your bills, do not stop praising yet because the enemy could come in and blindside you to put you further behind in your finances if you are not braced up. When your prodigal comes home, do not stop praying for him or her at that point!

Bracing yourself is sort of like girding yourself. Peter tells us to "gird up the loins of your mind, be sober, and rest your hope fully upon the grace that is to be brought to you at the revelation of Jesus Christ" (1 Peter 1:13). The Passion Translation puts it this way: "So then, prepare your hearts and minds for action! Stay alert and fix your hope firmly on the marvelous grace that is coming to you. For when Jesus Christ is unveiled, a greater measure of grace will be released to you."

Bracing yourself is basically staying alert in the spirit. Over and over we see warnings in Scripture about staying alert, and many times it is due to enemy activity. Peter again warns us: "Be well balanced and always alert, because your enemy, the devil, roams around incessantly, like a roaring lion looking for its prey to devour" (1 Peter 5:8 TPT). In the context of spiritual warfare, Paul admonishes us to pray "always with all prayer and supplication in the Spirit, being watchful to this end with all perseverance and supplication for all the saints" (Ephesians 6:18).

Bracing yourself means staying prayerful. Bracing yourself means thinking about what you are thinking about— being aware of your thoughts, because the enemy comes in with vain imaginations that exalt themselves against the knowledge of God (see 2 Corinthians 10:5). Bracing yourself means surrounding yourself with prayer warriors who will stand and withstand the backlash with you. Bracing yourself means staying in the Word, staying in community and staying in faith.

Stay Thanked Up!

Bracing yourself also means watching your mouth! Beyond staying prayed up, stay thanked up. The very mouth you used to release the sound of now can release the sound of death and open the door for the enemy to rain on your breakthrough parade. Staying in an attitude of thankfulness for the breakthrough helps you keep the breakthrough. Live in a state of gratitude to God that creates a spiritual climate over your life and attracts the Holy Spirit.

Remember the account of the ten lepers who saw Jesus approaching? These ten outcasts all let loose the sound of now:

> And they lifted up their voices and said, "Jesus, Master, have mercy on us!"
>
> So when He saw them, He said to them, "Go, show yourselves to the priests." And so it was that as they went, they were cleansed.
>
> And one of them, when he saw that he was healed, returned, and with a loud voice glorified God, and fell down on his face at His feet, giving Him thanks. And he was a Samaritan.
>
> So Jesus answered and said, "Were there not ten cleansed? But where are the nine? Were there not any found who returned to give glory to God except this foreigner?" And He said to him, "Arise, go your way. Your faith has made you well."
>
> Luke 17:13–19

The Holy Spirit decided to make a point in Scripture of the fact that only one of the ten lepers came back to say thank you. I have always wondered if those other nine lepers kept their miracle breakthroughs. Be careful not to do all the work to praise Him in advance and then forget to praise Him with that same level of fervor—that same sound—after the breakthrough. I do not want to press and push and sweat for a breakthrough and then go to coast mode after the breakthrough and lose what I gained.

If we are supposed to give thanks in all circumstances—even in trials—then how much more should we give thanks after a breakthrough! Let me put it to you this way: Your sound of now after the breakthrough should be the sound of thanks. Every time you think about what the Lord has done, thank Him.

So while you are alert in prayer, do the second part of Colossians 4:2: Magnify Him with thanksgiving. Your gratitude becomes a testimony to the goodness of God and acts as a shield against demonic suggestions.

Beyond all this, whatever you did to get the breakthrough, keep doing it! Develop a lifestyle of pressing into the presence of God and understand that the enemy is not giving up the fight just yet. The devil knows his time is short to steal your breakthrough—most breakthrough losses tend to happen in the first few weeks. Be assured the enemy will come back with a vengeance maybe sooner than you think; old enemies sometimes resurface to see how firmly you are standing in your miracle.

Do not fear backlash. Just know it is coming. Half the battle is knowing it is coming. When hurricanes threaten my south Florida shores, I never panic; I prepare. And remember, all breakthrough happens from the inside out. The sound of now comes from the inside and is expressed outwardly. The sound you make after the breakthrough may be different from the sound you made while waiting for God to move, but do not remain silent in the victory. Pray, dance, jump, shout, cry tears of joy—and stay alert in the Spirit.

When you meet with resistance, be encouraged. God heard your sound of now, but so did the enemy. He may try to get you to back down from your position of victory by faith in Christ. He may try to get you to forfeit your miracle. But your sound of now has already reached the throne, and angels are warring to bring the answer. When you have done all you can do, when you have released the sound of now, stand.

Notes

Chapter 1: The Sound of Now

1. All dictionary references for English words come from *Merriam-Webster's Collegiate Dictionary*. An online resource can be found at https://www.merriam-webster.com/.

2. William Branham, "Desperations," Church Ages, September 1, 1963, https://churchages.net/en/sermon/branham/63-0901E-desperations.

Chapter 2: The Art and Science of Sound

1. "Movie & Video Production Industry in the US—Market Research Report," IBISWorld, July 2020, https://www.ibisworld.com/united-states/market-research-reports/movie-video-production-industry/.

2. Ella Delany, "The Power of Sound as an Art Form," *New York Times*, October 3, 2013, https://www.nytimes.com/2013/10/04/arts/international/The-Power-of-Sound-as-an-Art-Form.html.

3. Colleen Vanderlinden, "It's True—You Really Should Talk to Your Plants," The Spruce, October 18, 2019, https://www.thespruce.com/should-you-talk-to-your-plants-3972298; Jo Tweedy, "Bizarre Experiment," *Daily Mail*, May 9, 2018, https://www.dailymail.co.uk/femail/article-5703247/Bizarre-experiment-shows-talking-plants-thrive.html.

4. Office Masaru Emoto, "Science of Water," accessed February 24, 2020, https://www.masaru-emoto.net/en/science-of-messages-from-water/.

5. TPS, "Heart Surgery in Jerusalem Performed Using Sound Waves," United with Israel, December 9, 2019, https://unitedwithisrael.org/israeli-first-heart-surgery-conducted-using-sound-waves/.

6. An online resource for *The KJV New Testament Greek Lexicon* can be found at https://www.biblestudytools.com/lexicons/greek/kjv/.

7. An online resource for *Strong's Exhaustive Concordance* can be found at https://www.biblestudytools.com/concordances/strongs-exhaustive-concordance/.

8. Kenneth E. Hagin, "Five Things God Wants to Do for You," Kenneth Hagin Ministries, accessed February 24, 2020, https://rhema.org/index.php?option=com_content&view=article&id=258:five-things-god-wants-to-do-for-you&catid=50&Itemid=457.

Chapter 3: Discovering the Sound of God

1. Oswald Chambers, "God's Silence—Then What?," *My Utmost for His Highest* (Grand Rapids: Discovery House, 1992).

Chapter 4: Engaging a Sound-Activated Kingdom

1. For more information, please see my book *The Year of the Decree* (Awakening Media, 2019).

Chapter 7: Discerning the Sound of War

1. For more about combating this destructive spirit, please see my book *The Spiritual Warrior's Guide to Defeating Jezebel* (Chosen, 2013).

2. St. Ignatius of Loyola, *The Spiritual Exercises of St. Ignatius of Loyola* (Boston: Digireads.com Publishing, 2018), 73.

Chapter 9: The Sound of Now Breaks Down Barriers to Your Promised Land

1. An online resource for *The KJV Hebrew Old Testament Lexicon* can be found at https://www.biblestudytools.com/lexicons/hebrew/kjv/.

Chapter 10: The Sound of Now in Music Brings Healing and Deliverance

1. Samuel Garrett, "The Healing Power of Music: Johns Hopkins Center Marries Music and Medicine," Johns Hopkins Medicine, n.d., https://www.artsandmindlab.org/the-healing-power-of-music-johns-hopkins-center-music-and-medicine/.

2. Beverly Merz, "Healing through Music," Harvard Health Publishing, November 5, 2015, https://www.health.harvard.edu/blog/healing-through-music-201511058556.

3. Amy Novotney, "Music As Medicine," American Psychological Association, November 2013, https://www.apa.org/monitor/2013/11/music.

4. Ashford University Staff, "How Does Music Affect Your Brain?," Ashford University, June 7, 2017, https://www.ashford.edu/online-degrees /student-lifestyle/how-does-music-affect-your-brain.

Chapter 11: The Sound of Now Births the New Thing

1. James W. Goll, *The Prophetic Intercessor: Releasing God's Purposes to Change Lives and Influence Nations* (Minneapolis: Chosen, 2007), 67.

2. Dutch Sheets, *Intercessory Prayer: How God Can Use Your Prayers to Move Heaven and Earth* (Minneapolis: Bethany, 1996), 143.

3. Cindy Jacobs, *Possessing the Gates of the Enemy: A Training Manual for Militant Intercession*, 4th ed. (Minneapolis: Chosen, 2018), 114.

Chapter 13: When the Sound of Now Is Tears

1. Joseph S. Exell and Henry Donald Maurice Spence-Jones, "Psalm 39:12," *The Pulpit Commentary*, Bible Hub, accessed April 20, 2020, https://biblehub.com/commentaries/psalms/39-12.htm.

Chapter 16: Releasing the Sound of Now in Intercession

1. Norman P. Grubb, *Rees Howells, Intercessor* (Cambridge: Lutterworth Press, 2013), 172.

2. Grubb, 172.

3. Grubb, 172.

Chapter 17: Many Manifestations of the Sound of Now

1. Matthew Henry, "Judges 16," *Concise Commentary on the Whole Bible*, Bible Hub, accessed April 21, 2020, https://biblehub.com/comment aries/mhc/judges/16.htm.

Jennifer LeClaire is a conference speaker, internationally recognized author and apostolic-prophetic voice to her generation. She inspires and challenges believers to pursue intimacy with God, cultivate their spiritual gifts and walk in the fullness of what God has called them to do. Jennifer contends for awakening in the nations through intercession and spiritual warfare, strong apostolic preaching and practical prophetic teaching that equips the saints for the work of the ministry.

Jennifer is the senior leader of Awakening House of Prayer in Fort Lauderdale, Florida, founder of Ignite Network and founder of the Awakening Prayer Hubs prayer movement.

Jennifer formerly served as the first editor of *Charisma* magazine, and she has written more than fifty books, including *The Making of a Prophet*, *The Spiritual Warrior's Guide to Defeating Jezebel*, *Satan's Deadly Trio*, *The Heart of the Prophetic*, *Mornings with the Holy Spirit* and *The Spiritual Warfare Battle Plan*. Some of her work has been translated into Spanish and Korean, and some is archived in the Flower Pentecostal Heritage Museum.

Beyond frequent appearances on The Elijah List, Jennifer writes one of *Charisma*'s most popular prophetic columns, *The Plumb Line*, and contributes often to *Charisma*'s *Prophetic Insight* newsletter. She has been interviewed on several media outlets, including *USA Today*, BBC, CBN, Sid Roth's *It's Supernatural!*, *Bill Martinez Live*, *Babbie's House* and *Atlanta Live*.

More from Jennifer LeClaire

In this book, leading prophetic voice Jennifer LeClaire guides readers along the journey of a prophet—from the initial call all the way through to maturity. Offering honest, accessible counsel to help you move into your prophetic calling, her spiritual insights will help you pursue true intimacy with God.

The Making of a Prophet

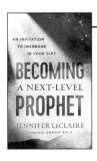

This empowering call to action—a helpful guide for the prophetically gifted—encourages both experienced and aspiring prophets to mature in their anointing and be good stewards of the gifts God has entrusted to them. It's crucial for God's prophets to rise up in this hour and declare with faithfulness what He is saying to this generation.

Becoming a Next-Level Prophet

You May Also Like . . .

Through Scripture, prophetic insight and practical experience, Jennifer LeClaire roots out the underlying workings of the spirit of control, idolatry and immorality to show you how to identify the true enemy and engage in effective warfare. Here are the weapons you need to battle the Jezebel deception—and win.

The Spiritual Warrior's Guide to Defeating Jezebel
by Jennifer LeClaire

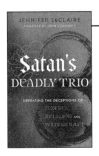

Veteran spiritual warrior Jennifer LeClaire pulls back the curtain on the calculated and systematic strategies of the enemy while offering practical biblical tactics to combat this deadly trio. Her Spirit-anointed discernment will help you to understand the hidden schemes of these evil spirits and, with God's help, resist them and live in victory.

Satan's Deadly Trio
by Jennifer LeClaire